American Folk Art

American Folk Art

BY

ELLEN S. SABINE

DRAWINGS BY THE AUTHOR

COLOR PHOTOGRAPHS
BY HILDA BORCHERDING

D. VAN NOSTRAND COMPANY, INC.

PRINCETON, NEW JERSEY

TORONTO   LONDON

NEW YORK

D. VAN NOSTRAND COMPANY, INC.
120 Alexander St., Princeton, New Jersey (*Principal office*)
257 Fourth Avenue, New York 10, New York

D. VAN NOSTRAND COMPANY, LTD.
358, Kensington High Street, London, W.14, England

D. VAN NOSTRAND COMPANY, (Canada), LTD.
25 Hollinger Road, Toronto 16, Canada

Published simultaneously in Canada by
D. VAN NOSTRAND COMPANY (Canada), LTD.

Library of Congress Catalogue Card No. 58-13834

PRINTED IN THE UNITED STATES OF AMERICA

Preface

The old decorative patterns used by American craftsmen, in the days when life was simpler and less mechanized, have not lost their beauty with the passing of time. This heritage has a timeless appeal, and today more and more people are finding relaxation and joy in adorning their homes with these fascinating designs, created anew by their own hands.

Folk art is a hobby that can be enjoyed both by the young and old; indeed, parents and children can work together on folk art projects with the happiest and most satisfying results. No elaborate art training is needed. The folk artist begins to produce acceptable work almost from the start, and progress is encouraged all the time by real achievement. At the same time, a naturally creative artist, one whose main expression might be in another field of art, learns valuable lessons from folk art techniques, with a resulting enrichment of his natural gifts. The young and growing mind inevitably acquires by the practice of folk art an appreciation of honest form and of the beauty of color; and it would not be out of place if some instruction in our historic American Folk Art formed part of the curriculum of every public school. The desire for the beautiful, inborn in every child, would be enhanced in a wholesome and constructive way.

Folk art, then, is not the exclusive preserve of highly trained professional artists, aiming to meet the tastes of connoisseurs and wealthy buyers. It could not be defined better than in these words, borrowed from William Morris, English poet and decorator of the last century: "Art made by the people and for the people as a joy to the maker and the user."

ACKNOWLEDGMENTS

For permission to use designs, for aid in gathering material, or for other assistance in preparing this book, I gratefully thank Mrs. Hedy Backlin, Mr. James Biddle, Mrs. Julia Borcherding, Miss Hilda M. Borcherding, Brooklyn Museum (Brooklyn, N.Y.), Mr. and Mrs. Vernon H. Brown, Mr. Arthur B. Carlson, Cooper Union Museum (New York), Miss Mary Aileen Dunne, Mr. Joseph Farrell, Free Library of Philadelphia, Index of American Design (National Gallery of Art, Washington, D.C.), Irene L. Lovett Antiques (New York), Mr. Abe E. Kessler, Mrs. Huldah Cail Lorimer, Mrs. John G. McTernan, Metropolitan Museum of Art (New York), New-York Historical Society, New York Public Library, Pennsylvania German Society (publishers of the late Dr. Henry S. Bornemann's classic *Pennsylvania German Illuminated Manuscripts*), Professor Harry W. Pfund, Queens Borough Public Library (Jamaica, N.Y.), Mr. Edward W. Schlechter, Mr. Marvin Schwartz, Miss Carolyn Scoon, Mrs. Jessie Van Doren, Mrs. Marion Wood, and my husband.

Contents

List of Illustrations

LINE PLATES

PHOTOGRAPHS

COLOR PLATES FROM FRAKTUR PAINTINGS

COLOR PLATES FROM PHOTOGRAPHS

SKETCHES

1

A Glance at the Past

American folk art, like so many of our institutions, had its roots in Europe. Craftsmen among the settlers introduced the techniques and cultural motifs of their old homelands to the new country, and from the earliest colonial times articles made and decorated in Europe were imported by colonial merchants and sold to the people. Thus the training of our native-born craftsmen was naturally and inevitably based on the art of England, France, and Germany, and the countries to which those three in turn owed so much.

Many kinds of art expression are embraced by the general term of "folk art," such as weaving, embroidery, pottery making, woodcarving, ornamental ironwork, painting, etc. Here we are concerned with decorative painting on furniture and smaller articles for household use, and also with the Fraktur painting which is such an outstanding part of American folk art.

Contrary to what many people suppose, the homes of an earlier period of our history were characterized by a liberal use of bright colors and cheerful designs. Floors were painted and decorated; walls were often tinted or stenciled, or were decorated with landscape paintings. There were stenciled and embroidered bedspreads, bright woven fabrics, decorated clocks and mirrors, painted furniture, boxes, trays, and other useful items. All these things gave an air of brightness and individuality to homes.

The flourishing period of American folk art was from about the middle of the 18th century to the time of the Civil War. It was then practiced consistently and on a considerable scale in the older parts of the country, notably in the rural communities of New England and Pennsylvania. The folk craftsmen favored traditional motifs, introducing modifications as the need arose or as fancy suggested. And that, let us note, is just what we today find ourselves doing as we follow in their footsteps. We respect tradition, but we are not its prisoners.

[*1*]

Connecticut craftsmen probably produced the earliest pieces of decorated furniture, such as chests, highboys, chairs, and boxes. At first, the carpenter or joiner who made the furniture also painted the decoration; later on, coach and sign painters found it profitable to turn their hands to decorating household furniture, the demand for which was continually increasing.

Utensils of tinware decorated with folk art motifs were very popular. Sheets of tinplate (iron that was coated with tin) began to be imported from England in the mid 18th century, and American tinsmiths made it into coffee pots, tea pots, tea caddies, trays, canisters, candle holders, sconces, and many kinds of boxes, such as those for documents, trinkets, and candles. Such articles were also imported ready made. In meeting the demand for decorated ware, the tinsmith either employed an artist or turned that part of the work over to the artistically inclined members of his own family.

The finished pieces of tinware were mostly retailed by peddlers who traveled up and down the land, selling from door to door. Hence it is difficult to be sure just where the articles originated; but it is generally believed that most of them were made in Pennsylvania, Connecticut, and Maine. At first the tin peddler carried his wares on his back. Later he traveled on horseback and, with improving roads, was able to use a cart. In colonial times cash was not plentiful, paper money was disliked, and so the peddler was often glad to take farm produce in exchange for his tinware. His arrival at a farm or hamlet was quite a notable occasion, for besides the brightly decorated wares he brought news and gossip from distant places.

A highly distinctive contribution made to American folk art was that of the Pennsylvania Germans. Refugees from religious and political troubles in their homeland, they settled in southeastern Pennsylvania, bringing with them the rich heritage of their native folk art. Dower chests, cupboards, dressers, benches, boxes of all kinds, and numerous other useful household objects were decorated in bright, gay colors with the designs characteristic of the Pennsylvania "Dutch," who, of course, were not Dutch at all, but German (or *Deutsch* in their own language). Since almost every Pennsylvania German maiden of marriageable age received a dower chest, whose painted decoration usually included her name and a date, it is not surprising that many of those beautiful chests have been carefully preserved by their descendants. Likewise, many bride boxes have come down to us, the bride box being the customary gift of a groom to his bride. It was used to hold the smaller items of her trousseau.

Besides these decorative arts, which were like those of other American communities, the Pennsylvania Germans brought here the unique art of *Fraktur-Schriften,* or the making of illuminated manuscripts. *Fraktur* is a German word meaning a certain design of 15th century Gothic letter, while *schriften* means "writing." The application of Fraktur was gradually expanded in common usage to cover both the design of the lettering and the colored embellishment of it. Eventually the term came to be applied not only to all manuscripts of the type, but also to the style of decoration even when it was unaccompanied by any writing.

Historically, Fraktur painting is a survival from the middle ages, when manuscript records and literary works were accompanied by more or less elaborate drawings or paintings in gold and color. The advent of printing with movable type in the 15th century gradually brought the making of manuscript books to an end, but in some places, and for limited purposes, the art of embellishing manuscripts was continued. In Germany the continued use of the Gothic black-letter for printing, as formerly for writing, encouraged the survival of the art. When the Germans arrived in Pennsylvania they brought the art with them, and it not merely survived there, but in the course of time developed into a form peculiar to the Pennsylvania "Dutch." It came to be an essential part of their cultural life, reaching the peak period of its cultivation between 1800 and 1840. It was used primarily for important documents like certificates of birth, baptism, and marriage; and also for bookplates, for pious inscriptions to hang on the wall as "house blessings," for valentines, and for decorations in song books.

It is significant that Fraktur painting was taught in the schools of the Pennsylvania Germans. A great variety of Fraktur designs were used as specimens to be copied in conjunction with the learning of penmanship; some were awarded to children as prizes; some were made just to display the skill of the schoolmaster himself. The teaching of Fraktur painting continued until the 1850's, when the English school system was established. It is not difficult to see the great influence of the formal teaching of Fraktur. It added to the skill of workers in various practical arts, such as pottery, ironware, joinery, embroidery, box painting, etc., and at the same time it put at their disposal a whole repertoire of art motifs. In all such crafts, Fraktur designs were used again and again.

[*3*]

After the Civil War the increasing standardization of life, including the employment of methods of mass production, put an end to the continuity of most folk art in American life. But the old craftsmen had scarcely passed from the scene before some of their descendants began to regret the loss of the knowledge and skill of which the treasured evidences still adorned their homes, alongside the products of the modern age. Gone were most of the old hardships and inconveniences, and a good thing too; but was it inevitable, people began to ask, to abandon arts which satisfy the inner need to create things of beauty with one's own hands? Some of them answered the query by setting to work reverently and painstakingly to revive the practice of the arts of their forefathers.

And so, after this brief glance at the past, we will turn to the means by which we too may recapture and enjoy the forms of American folk art with which this book deals.

PHOTO 1   CONNECTICUT CHEST, ca. 1705
(courtesy of the Metropolitan Museum of Art)

PHOTO 2   PENNSYLVANIA DOWER CHEST, ca. 1780   [5]
(courtesy of the Metropolitan Museum of Art)

PHOTO 3   PENNSYLVANIA DOWER CHEST, ca. 1800
(courtesy of the Metropolitan Museum of Art)

[6]   PHOTO 4   BLANKET CHEST FROM TAUNTON, MASSACHUSSETTS, ca. 1735
(courtesy of Metropolitan Museum of Art)

Photo 5   BRIDE BOX, CEDAR WOOD, 18TH CENTURY
          (courtesy of the Metropolitan Museum of Art)

Photo 6   PENNSYLVANIA CAP BOX, CEDAR WOOD, 18TH CENTURY   [7]
          (courtesy of the Metropolitan Museum of Art)

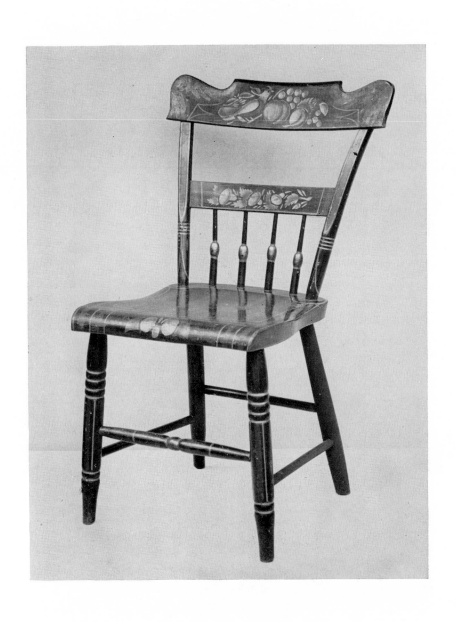

[8]   PHOTO 7   PENNSYLVANIA CHAIR, ca. 1825
(courtesy of the Metropolitan Museum of Art)

2

Materials and How to Care for Them

To begin with, we must have a list of those things which will be necessary in our work. Here is the list, together with instructions for the care of the materials, and (at the end of the chapter) the names of some recommended suppliers:

Tube Colors. (a) Japan Colors in tubes of Vermilion (light), Chrome Green (light), Chrome Yellow (medium), and Lamp Black.

(b) Artists' Oil Colors in small tubes of Alizarin Crimson, Prussian Blue, Burnt Sienna, Burnt Umber, Raw Umber, Yellow Ochre, and Indian Yellow or Yellow Lake; also a medium-sized tube of Titanium White or Superba White. Note that the Alizarin Crimson, Prussian Blue, Indian Yellow, and Yellow Lake differ from the others because they are transparent colors.

The Japan colors were originally ground in Japan and were used in the Western world by the old-time coach painters. They are opaque and, when dry, give a flat, smooth surface. The tubes in which the paint comes should be handled carefully, since they crack easily. When that happens the paint soon dries and is useless. When not in use the tubes should be left standing upside down, that is, with the cap at the bottom. Because the paint oil will rise in the tube, this position tends to keep the oil mixed with the pigment, and avoids oil running out when you squeeze the tube for use. A tin can makes a good tube holder. See Plate 1.

Keep the caps screwed on all tubes when they are not in actual use. If a cap sticks, don't try to unscrew it by using force which would twist the tube. Instead, hold the cap, for a few seconds only, in the flame of a match. The warmth will cause the cap to expand, and using a cloth to protect your fingers, you can then unscrew it.

[*9*]

If paint does not emerge from the opening of tube when you try to squeeze some out, do not apply so much pressure that the tube itself splits. Probably some dried paint is clogging the opening, and this can be lifted out with a narrow knife blade.

Varnish. Varnish is used as a medium for mixing tube colors in the painting of designs, and for the finishing coats on a decorated piece. Pratt & Lambert #61 Floor Varnish, clear gloss, is a good quality varnish which I use with good results. Whenever varnish is mentioned in this book, that is the quality of varnish intended, unless otherwise indicated. A number of other fine varnishes are on the market which expert decorators have found to work beautifully, among them McCloskey's, Murphy's, Pierce's. Very heavy varnishes are not good for our work.

Varnish should never be stirred. The half pint size is handiest. So long as the can has not been opened, the contents will keep in a perfect state. On contact with the air, the spirits begin to evaporate, and once the varnish shows signs of definite thickening, it should not be used. Since varnish cannot be salvaged, proper care should be taken from the first to ensure that no needless waste occurs. It is obvious that the cover should be kept on the can when the varnish is not in use. Be sure, however, that the cover is on *tightly*—step on it to make quite sure. When about one-third of the varnish has been used, it is a good plan to pour the remainder into small bottles which can be filled to the top and covered with good screw caps. The idea is to expose the varnish to as little air as possible. Even though it is tightly covered, the air, even in a one-third empty can, will thicken the varnish.

Primer. A high-grade metal primer paint which dries smooth and thus requires very little sandpapering should be used. It should be stirred thoroughly before use. Pratt & Lambert's Effecto Enamel Primer is among the better-grade primer paints, and it may be thinned with turpentine.

When you have finished using the paint, wipe off any excess paint in the rim of the can with a cloth. Then pour a little turpentine on top of the paint in the can, just enough to cover the surface, letting it float there. The turpentine will prevent a skin forming on the surface of the paint. Then replace the can lid and press it down tightly. The next time you open the can, simply mix the turpentine in with the paint, and it will probably thin it just enough for use.

Background Paints. For flat black background painting, Pratt & Lambert's Sta-Blac *Flat* Enamel is an excellent, well-covering paint. It should be cared for in the same way as the primer. Sherwin-Williams,

Lowe, and Sapolin are among other makers of high-quality flat black paints.

For flat background colors, see Chapter 6 (How to Mix Background Colors).

Black Drawing Ink.

Crow-quill Pen. A fine-pointed pen.

Drawing Pencils. H, 2H, and 4H.

Decorator's Masking Tape. One roll.

Frosted Acetate. One roll, medium weight. This is a transparent plastic sheet, one side of which is slightly frosted so that it will take paint. Its transparency enables one directly to copy a pattern placed under the acetate sheet, without having first to trace an outline.

Tracing Paper. One roll 21 inches wide, thin and very transparent.

Brushes. (a) For applying coats of varnish and background paints, ordinary one-inch flat bristle brushes as sold for a small price in paint stores can be used. Some decorators, however, prefer to use better-quality brushes for this work, and find them worth the extra cost. In any event, it is of the first importance to keep the brush in perfect condition.

To clean a flat bristle brush, first wipe it off thoroughly on newspaper. Then douse it up and down in turpentine, and let it stand for 15 minutes in enough of the fluid to cover the hairs. (This turpentine can be kept in a screw-top jar and used several times over.) Then wash the brush thoroughly in warm (not hot) water, and rinse well. Shake out surplus water, and shape the brush carefully. Stand it up on the handle in a jar where it can dry undisturbed.

If you intend to use a *paint* brush again the next day, it need not be cleaned, but may be left standing overnight in turpentine or in plain water, provided there is enough liquid in the jar to cover the hairs and provided the brush is suspended so that it does not rest on the hairs. A *varnish* brush, however, must be cleaned each time it is used.

(b) For painting designs we require these more specialized types of brushes: (1) *Square-tipped ox-hair rigger or showcard brushes* #5 or 6 in certain makes (but not in all, so consult the actual-size drawings of this and the following brush given in Plate 1). The hairs should be 5/8 to 3/4 inch long. Buy two for convenience. (2) *Square-tipped camel's hair quill brushes,* #0 and #1 in some makes. Hairs should be 3/4 inch long. (3) *Striper.* This is a square-tipped quill brush with hairs about 1½ inches long, and about the thickness of a #1 quill. It is used without a handle.

To clean these smaller brushes, wipe them gently with a cloth, and then douse them up and down in Carbona Cleaning Fluid or carbon tetrachloride. Let them stand in the fluid about 15 minutes, so that any paint that has worked up into the ferrule is dissolved. Then wash thoroughly in soap and water, and rinse. Shake out surplus water, shape the brush carefully, and stand the brushes on their handles in a jar undisturbed until they are dry.

It is only at the end of a painting session that you wash the brush in soap and water as described above, since you cannot paint properly with a brush that is still wet from water. Therefore, when you have finished painting in one color, and want to go on at once and paint in the next color, clean the brush thoroughly and promptly in Carbona only.

Cotton Rags. For wiping up paint or wiping brushes, cotton is best.

Plastic Wood.

Paint and Varnish Remover.

Shellac. This, like the two previous items, is obtainable in the paint stores. Always use fresh shellac. Shellac left over from previous jobs or shellac left standing in half-empty jars for a while should not be used. The shellac will probably not dry properly, but remain sticky, and then your only recourse is to remove it with the paint and varnish remover— a disagreeable and time-wasting job.

Turpentine. One quart. Give can a shake or two before using.

Steel Wool. #000. Buy it in a paint store.

Sandpaper. #000 or very fine.

Crude Oil. Pint bottle can be bought from paint store.

Carbona Cleaning Fluid. One bottle. Examine label carefully for this exact wording: "Carbona Cleaning Fluid," because the Carbona company makes other cleaners useless for our purpose.

Powdered Pumice. 2-oz. size. Can be bought at a drug store or hardware store.

Magnesium Carbonate. 1-oz. cake, usually available at the larger drug stores.

Rusticide, or *Deoxidine.* For removing rust. Rusticide is sometimes procurable in hardware or paint stores, or a bottle can be bought direct from the Rusticide Products Co., 3125 Perkins Avenue, Cleveland 14, Ohio. Deoxidine is available only in quart or larger sizes, and is not sold in stores. Write to Amchen Products, Inc., Ambler, Pennsylvania for the address of your nearest distributor. See "Removing Rust" in Chapter 5 for directions.

Bottle Caps. Start saving bottle caps about one inch in diameter and ½ inch high—for example, those that come on catsup bottles. Bottle caps make convenient-sized receptacles for varnish used in painting designs.

Empty Jars and Bottles. Collect some small jars or bottles, about 2 or 3 inches deep, with good, airtight screw tops. These will be needed for holding varnish and Carbona Cleaning Fluid. Cold-cream jars and others of similar type are useful for holding the mixed background colors.

Newspapers. Always have plenty of newspapers on hand. You will need them to spread over your work tables, to wipe brushes, and to use as "palettes" in painting designs.

HANDY LIST OF SOME SUPPLIERS

Many artist supply stores carry items which are used by the American Folk Art decorator. For your convenience, the following is a list of some of the suppliers. Several of these carry trays and woodware. Some issue a catalog of their stock items. All will gladly answer your enquiries.

Joseph Mayer Co., 5-9 Union Square West, New York 3, N.Y.
Empire Artists' Materials, 135 East 60 Street, New York 22, N.Y.
Arthur Brown, 2 West 46th Street, New York 36, N.Y.
E. P. Lynch, Inc., 92 Weybosset Street, Providence, R.I. (catalog).
Block Artists' Materials, 72 Weybosset Street, Providence, R.I. (catalog).
Brenner's Paint Shop, 8 Samoset Street, Plymouth, Mass.
The Stone Co., 19-21 Elm Street, Danbury, Conn.
M. M. Ross Co. Art Supply, 72 Huntington Avenue, Boston 16, Mass. (catalog).
The Country Loft, Newfields, N.H. (catalog).*
Crafts Mfg. Co., Lunenburg, Mass. (catalog).*
Hoitt & Wentworth, 559 Central Avenue, Dover, N.H. (catalog).*
Colonial Handcraft Trays, New Market, Virginia (catalog).*
Village Tin Shop, 1030 Main Street, Hingham, Mass.: (catalog).*

* These firms specialize in tin and woodenware.

3

How to Use the Brush in Painting Designs

What is the first thing you do in learning the art of decorating objects? Do you take a piece of furniture or tinware and go right to work on it? No! Experience has shown again and again that before you do that you must practice the brush strokes, and you must practice painting patterns. The former is done on paper, and the latter on sheets of frosted acetate (see p. 17). When you have learned in those ways how to handle the brushes, and how to apply color in the painting of designs, you will be better able to start on an actual object. You won't spoil the object, and you will be much happier about the result of your first piece of work than if you went at it without the previous practice.

Before starting the brush stroke practice, the necessary items must be assembled. The work must be done on a table which is not too high for you. A card table has a good height for most people. Protect the top with several sheets of newspaper. This table will be used for all our painting practice.

Take a double sheet of newspaper, and fold it into eighths so as to make a handy "palette." Newspaper is used because it has the advantage of absorbing superfluous oil in the paint. The other things you will need are these:

A small bottle-cap filled with varnish.

A tube of Japan Vermilion.

A square-tipped showcard brush for mixing.

A square-tipped camel's-hair quill brush for painting.

Some tracing paper.

A small jar half full of Carbona Cleaning Fluid for cleaning the brushes.

Some paint rags (cotton).

Brush Strokes in Plate 1

With the items just listed now available, you are ready to begin practicing the brush strokes. Place a piece of tracing paper over Plate 1. Squeeze out a little color on the newspaper palette, and dip out some varnish onto it with the showcard brush. With the showcard brush, mix the varnish with the color. The mixture should contain enough varnish to make it easily manageable, and yet it must not be so thin that it spreads once it has been painted. It should be thoroughly mixed, so that no lumps of paint remain.

Dip the quill brush into this mixture, and then work the brush back and forth once or twice on the palette to work the paint into the hairs. The object is to load the brush to its full length, and not just the tip of it. Avoid overloading—the brush should not be dripping or bulging with paint.

Now hold the brush as illustrated in Plate 1, that is, almost vertically, but with a very slight inclination towards you. The wrist should be off the surface, with the hand resting lightly on the tip of the little finger. Rest the forearm on the edge of the table.

Paint the broad stripe at the top of the Plate, as seen through the tracing paper. Observe how the brush flattens out to a knife-edge once it is lowered. Next, slowly raising the brush, pull it off and down to one side, using the knife-edge to end the stroke on a hairline.

Proceed to paint the rows of brush strokes in the illustration, starting at the broad end of each stroke, and gradually raising the brush to end on a hairline. Paint each stroke slowly and deliberately. If your stroke finishes too thick, either you had too much paint mixture on the brush or you did not raise the brush enough. Too much paint on the brush may also cause the strokes to spread a few minutes after you have painted them.

Except for very small strokes, reload the brush for each stroke, always reloading to the full length of the hairs. With practice you will learn to load the brush instinctively with just the right amount of paint for the size of stroke you desire. If the brush becomes so flattened that you get a stroke like the one marked X, turn the brush slightly, so that, as you put it down on the pattern, the hairs round themselves for the start of the stroke.

For a stroke that starts on a point and ends on a point, flatten the brush on the newspaper palette, and then, holding the brush high, begin the stroke; lower the brush to do the broad part of the stroke,

[*15*]

X

CAMEL-HAIR
QUILL
(ACTUAL SIZE)

SHOWCARD
BRUSH
(ACTUAL
SIZE)

PLATE 1   BRUSH STROKE PRACTICE AND CEDAR WOOD BOX PATTERN

and finally lift it to complete the stroke. For a thin line or vein, flatten the brush on the newspaper and then paint with the knife-like edge. For a dot, round the brush on the newspaper, and then holding the brush high, paint the dot with the end of the brush.

Whenever the paint begins to thicken, clean the brush in Carbona Cleaning Fluid. Squeeze out a little fresh paint, and mix with varnish on another part of the newspaper.

Don't hesitate to turn your work round to any convenient angle that suits the particular stroke you are doing; rotate the work completely around if necessary. It is a good plan to use your left hand to shift the pattern about all the time, so as to suit the work to every new stroke you make; thus you will always be at a comfortable angle for each stroke. Patience and practice will do the rest. By practicing half an hour every day for a week or two, you should acquire a fair command of the brush.

Tea Caddy Pattern on Plate 2

To make a duplicate of the tea caddy pattern on Plate 2, cut a piece of frosted acetate large enough for the design, and attach it by three of its corners to a piece of thin cardboard. Use small pieces of decorator's tape to fasten the corners. Slip this contrivance into the book in the manner shown in the drawing on Plate 1. In this way, you will have brought the tea caddy pattern under the acetate. By painting the pattern directly on the acetate, you will get not merely a color record of it, but also valuable practice at the same time. See the Cornucopia pattern in Color Plate IX for the colors, which are similar to those for the tea caddy indicated in the legend. The step-by-step procedure for painting the tea caddy pattern follows.

1. On a newspaper palette squeeze out a little Japan Vermilion. Using the showcard brush, dip several brushfuls of varnish out of the bottle-cap, and mix them with a small quantity of the color. Paint the large flower and the buds marked V, disregarding the overtone strokes. The paint should be opaque, but yet contain sufficient varnish for it to dry smooth and flat. Clean the brush by wiping off the excess paint on a rag, and then dipping it in Carbona.

2. Squeeze out a little Japan Green and a tiny bit of Burnt Umber. With the showcard brush, mix some Green, adding a speck of Burnt Umber to tone down the Green a little. With this "country green" mixture, paint those "leaves" which are shown black in the illustration, using your quill brush for this purpose.

[*17*]

V   VERMILION
   COUNTRY GREEN
LG   LIGHT COUNTRY GREEN
/////   DARK TRANSPARENT RED
Y   MUSTARD YELLOW
::::   THIN OFF-WHITE

PLATE 2   TEA CADDY AND COFFEE POT

3. Squeeze out a little Japan Yellow and add a touch of it to the green mixture, making a much lighter and yellower green. With this mixture, paint the leaves, which are shown white in the illustration. Remove the cardboard and acetate from the book, and set it aside to dry for 24 hours.

4. To paint the shaded and dotted overtones on the vermilion flower, do not put the acetate back over the illustration. These are done by eye, using the illustration as a guide. On a clean palette mix several brushfuls of varnish with a little Alizarin Crimson and a touch of Burnt Umber, making a rich, dark, semi-transparent red. With this mixture, and using the showcard brush, paint in the line-shaded area on the flower. Only one or two broad strokes should be used. Don't fuss over it. Do it once and leave it.

Immediately that this is done, take a camel's-hair quill brush, dip it in the varnish, and wipe off some of the varnish on the newspaper palette, at the same time flattening the brush. Now, with one stroke, draw the flattened brush along the inner edge of the dark overtone, with the brush partly on the red and partly off. This will blend and soften the edge of the dark red, giving the flower a softly shaded look. If you don't get it just right the first time, you may *immediately* wipe it off with a clean cotton cloth; possibly a little clean Carbona on the cloth may be necessary. But the wiping must be done at once, before the color sets.

If you use too much varnish on the blending brush, it will spread and disturb the smooth appearance of the dark red. Practice tells you just how much to use each time. While you are using the dark red color, do not overlook the large oval dot.

Proceed to mix some Japan Yellow with a little Burnt Umber, making a rich mustard yellow, and with this paint the dots arranged in rings. Add more varnish to the mustard, to make it semi-transparent, and paint the strokes on the green leaves indicated by the dotted white lines. Wait 24 hours.

5. For the dotted overtone strokes, mix some varnish with a little White, and add a touch of Raw Umber to make a semi-transparent off-white overtone. Where this is painted on the vermilion flower, it will take on a fairly pinkish tone. Set aside to dry for 24 hours.

The background color on the original tea caddy was a dark brown asphaltum. But black makes just as suitable a background, and is much easier to do. The use of asphaltum backgrounds need not occupy us at this point (being described later at p. 34), but it may be of interest to

[*19*]

mention that the Color Plate V illustrates two pieces of old tinware which have asphaltum backgrounds. The patterns of these two pieces may be seen in my book *American Antique Decoration.*

Coffee Pot Pattern on Plate 2

This pattern is very like the one described above, but the leaf strokes shown white in the drawing are to be painted in mustard yellow. The crosshatching and the curlicues also are to be done in mustard yellow. To do the crosshatching, pick up very little paint on the quill brush, flatten the brush on the newspaper, and paint the lines with the knife-like edge thus obtained. Curlicues are best done with a smaller quill brush (#0), using very little paint on the brush, and holding the brush high to paint with just the tip of the hairs. It takes a fair amount of practice to do these well. The dots are in vermilion. The original background was asphaltum.

Refer to the Group of Old Boxes and Country Tinware in Sketch Plate A (p. 85) for the position of the design on the coffee pot.

Important Note

Before proceeding to describe the painting of the next pattern it may be well to repeat the important rule which applies to all our painting work: Let one color dry thoroughly before painting another color over it. The minimum drying time is always 24 hours.

Cedar Wood Box on Plate 1

1. Squeeze out a little Prussian Blue, some Raw Umber, and some White. Mix these together to get a rather dark blue, bearing in mind that Prussian Blue is a powerful color, and that a little of it goes a long way. Also be careful not to add too much Umber, since that would make the color muddy-looking, instead of the rich, soft blue we are seeking. With this blue, paint all those parts of the design which are black in the illustration. Wait 24 hours.

2. Squeeze out a little Japan Yellow, a little Raw Umber, and a touch of White. Mix these to form a pale mustard yellow. Paint those parts of the design marked Y. Wait 24 hours.

3. Mix White with a touch of Raw Umber to get off-white, and paint the remaining parts of the design.

This design was taken from a natural color cedarwood Trinket Box. At a later stage in the work, if you should wish to decorate a box with this design, you may reproduce the color of the original background by mixing White, Burnt Umber, and a touch of Yellow Ochre.

Additional Practice

At this point, you will probably have begun to realize how valuable and enjoyable your practice in painting designs can be. So for more practice, turn to one or more of these Plates: 7, 8, 13, 23, 27, 28, 29, 31. Any or all of these may be copied at this stage with the assurance that you are making yourself more skillful with the brush all the time.

Preserving Patterns

When a pattern is completed and thoroughly dry, mount it on a piece of thin cardboard or heavy paper, if possible of the same color as the background of the original. The mounting is done by attaching the pattern at the corners with bits of cellophane tape, and the face of the pattern is protected by a wax-paper flap. Keep the patterns in a folder for future reference.

Color Key for Painted Patterns

Throughout this book we shall be dealing with colors and how to obtain them. Here then is a convenient key to the colors we shall be using. They are more or less standard colors in American antique designs and are arranged in groups for easier reference—the reds, the greens, the blues, the browns, yellow, and off-white. Rarely do we use bright color fresh from the tube. Indeed, with the exception of Vermilion, all the bright colors must be toned down by the addition of Yellow Ochre or one of the browns in order to obtain those beautiful, soft, antique shades that are so admired. Opposite each color in the list below are the tube colors by which it is obtained. Mix the colors with the showcard brush, using varnish as the medium. Of course, the colors must be mixed completely, so that no lumps of pigment remain.

Prefixed to each color is the letter or combination of letters by which it is indicated in the black-and-white drawings.

V	bright red	Japan Vermilion.
S	salmon pink	Japan Vermilion, Yellow Ochre, and a touch of White.
P	pale pink	As for salmon pink, but with more White added.
A	dark red overtone	Alizarin Crimson, with a touch of Burnt Umber and enough varnish to make a semi-transparent rich dark red.

G	country green	Japan Green, with a touch of Burnt Umber.
LG	light green	Japan Green with a little Japan Yellow, and a touch of Burnt Umber.
DG	dark country green	Japan Green, a touch of Raw Umber and Prussian Blue.
OG	olive green	Japan Green with a little Burnt Sienna.
YG	yellow green	Japan Yellow, a little Japan Green, and a touch of Raw Umber.
B	medium blue	Prussian Blue, with a little Raw Umber and White.
LB	light blue	White with a little Prussian Blue and Raw Umber.
DB	dark blue	Prussian Blue, with Raw Umber and a touch of White.
RU	dark brown	Raw Umber.
BU	medium brown	Burnt Umber.
BS	reddish brown	Burnt Sienna.
Y	mustard yellow	Japan Yellow, with Burnt Umber added a little at a time until you get the color you want. For a greenish mustard, use Raw Umber. For an orange mustard, use Burnt Sienna.
W	off-white	White with a touch of Raw Umber. For white overtones, use enough varnish to make the mixture semi-transparent.

Transparent Color Mixtures

From time to time, transparent and semi-transparent colors, or "overtones," are mentioned in the pages which follow. These are simply colors sufficiently thinned with varnish for a hint of the color underneath to show through. The degree of transparency will naturally vary according to the quantity of varnish. It is usually best to start with several brushfuls of varnish, adding a very little pigment at a time until you reach the proper consistency.

4

How to Prepare Wood for Decoration

It is wise to begin the work of decorating actual objects by choosing an article made of wood. Few jobs undertaken by the amateur craftsman give more delight and pride than converting a discarded, perhaps unattractive, piece of furniture into a thing of beauty by using one of our folk art patterns. An old chair, a coffee table, a chest of drawers, a wooden floor lamp, a tray, a box—these are some of the many articles which the folk artist transforms in ways that add new charm and individuality to the home.

Old Wood

To prepare old wood for decoration, proceed as follows:

1. Remove all old paint and varnish with any good brand of paint and varnish remover. Make a thorough job of it, because the preparation of a painting surface is as important as the decoration itself. Follow the directions on the can, and have plenty of old rags and newspapers at hand. Work with the windows open to prevent harmful inhalation of the fumes.

2. Fill in all holes and cracks with plastic wood. Let it dry.

3. Smooth the surface by sandpapering the flat parts and rubbing the rounded parts with steel wool.

4. You are now ready for the first background coat of paint. Spread out plenty of newspapers on your worktable.

Flat Background Painting

A properly painted background, whether black or any color, should be a completely flat or dull surface, feeling smooth and free from ridges when the hand is run over it. If you can feel any ridges, your paint was not sufficiently thinned with turpentine. To smooth the surface by sandpapering may take a great deal of time and hard work; therefore, if you apply the paint correctly in the first place, you will save yourself much trouble. With this preliminary word of caution in mind, the following directions should be studied and carefully followed.

The paint should be thinned with enough turpentine to make a very watery mixture. Usually there is not enough room in a fresh can of paint for the necessary amount of turpentine to thin the paint properly. Procure a small empty jar, and pour into it about a quarter of an inch of turpentine. After stirring the black paint in the can until it is thoroughly mixed, dip out one or two brushfuls, and add them to the turpentine in the jar. Mix with the brush. The resulting mixture should be quite thin and watery. Important: give the turpentine can a shake or two before using.

Before applying the paint, examine the object to be painted and decide which part you will paint first, which next, and so on. Also, find out how you will hold the object during the painting. Be sure to leave one part unpainted on which the object can rest while drying, and prepare the place beforehand on which you will set the object to dry. Think all this out *before* you apply the paint.

After dusting off the surface, apply the paint in long even strokes. Don't flood the paint on. Use just enough to cover the surface. Because of the thinner in the paint, the first coat will not cover the surface completely; but don't go back and retouch any part of it. Paint it and leave it. Check around the edges for any dripping. Allow 24 hours for drying.

When applying the second coat, paint any large areas in the opposite direction to the first coat, that is, apply the second coat crosswise. This method achieves an even result. The object should have at least three coats, preferably four. Never apply a second or later coat until the preceding one has dried for at least 24 hours and until it feels thoroughly dry.

Allow the final coat of paint to harden at least a week before doing a design on it. (A longer period of waiting, such as a month, is recommended, especially for the light or colored backgrounds you will do later on. It will be safer to make corrections with cleaning fluid on a completely hardened background). The waiting period can be usefully occupied by further practice with the brush, in painting patterns, or by preparing other pieces of furniture or household articles for decoration.

[*24*]

PHOTO 8   FRAKTUR, BIRTH AND BAPTISMAL CERTIFICATE, PENNSYLVANIA,
       18TH CENTURY   [25]
       (courtesy of the Metropolitan Museum of Art)

[26]   PHOTO 9   FRAKTUR, WATERCOLOR DRAWING, PENNSYLVANIA, 19TH CENTURY
(courtesy of the Metropolitan Museum of Art)

Photo 10   PENNSYLVANIA PLATE, ca. 1800
(courtesy of the Metropolitan Museum of Art)

Photo 11   PENNSYLVANIA PLATE, 18TH CENTURY   [27]
(courtesy of the Metropolitan Museum of Art)

Photo 12 pennsylvania plate, 19th century
(courtesy of the Metropolitan Museum of Art)

If you did a proper job of sandpapering and preparing the wood in the first place, and you have applied the paint as directed, you should now have a smooth, dull surface which needs no sanding.

If it is necessary, however, sandpaper the last coat *very lightly* with a square inch or so of fine sandpaper. A small piece can be controlled better than a large one. Avoid sandpapering edges and other "vulnerable" parts, by which is meant parts where the sandpaper would take the paint off altogether.

New Wood

In the case of new wood, the process of preparation is as follows:

1. Sandpaper well, first using fairly coarse paper, and then the finer kind. Use steel wool on the turned parts and on carving.

2. Fill in crevices with plastic wood. When it is dry, sandpaper again.

3. Apply a coat of shellac to seal the wood. Let it dry for 24 hours.

4. Sandpaper again.

5. Apply three or four coats of thin background paint in the way already described.

Mass Production

Fortunately, mass production in the usual sense of the term is not applicable to American folk art decoration! But I use the expression to convey an idea of the value of the economical use of time and effort. Practically never do I paint only one object at a time. By a little planning ahead you can generally arrange to carry several articles through the preparatory stages up to background painting. Then you can please yourself as to when you want to decorate them. Similarly, when the time comes to apply the finishing coats of varnish, it is very economical to wait until you have several pieces to do.

5

How to Prepare Tin for Decoration

Removing Old Paint or Varnish

The first step in preparing a surface for decoration is to remove all old paint or varnish, for which purpose any good brand of paint and varnish remover will do. To reduce the chance of inhaling the fumes, work with the windows open. Read and follow the directions on the can, and have plenty of rags and old newspapers close at hand.

Removing Rust

In its initial stages, rust is invisible to the naked eye, and therefore all tinware should be treated for rust whether it can be seen or not. To remove rust you may use Rusticide or Deoxidine (see p. 12 for addresses of manufacturers). Rusticide, which may be available in a hardware or paint store, comes in small bottles with directions for use. If the piece is badly rusted several applications of Rusticide may be necessary.

Clean off all remains of the Rusticide with a cleaning fluid. Then wash the tin object with soap and water, rinse well, and dry thoroughly. Without delay, proceed to apply the primer paint. Do not let the article stand for any length of time, for rust will begin to form again.

To use Deoxidine, dilute one part of Deoxidine with three parts of cold water, preparing only enough for the job in hand. With a paint brush, apply this solution to the tin, and leave on for five minutes. Rub the surface with steel wool, and give it a second application. After five minutes rub again with steel wool. Rinse the article thoroughly in cold water, dry it, and proceed to paint.

[*30*]

Primer Painting

A tin surface must always be given one or two coats of primer paint (see Chapter 2) before the background color is applied, or the latter will not adhere properly. Spread plenty of newspapers on the table or other working surface, and be sure the primer paint has been thoroughly mixed.

The first coat of primer paint is usually not thinned, although it may be thinned a little if it seems too thick. Apply it as you would a background coat of paint. The second coat of primer may be thinned a little with turpentine. On large flat surfaces it should be applied in a crosswise direction to the first coat. When completely dry, go over the surface with sandpaper to remove any tiny "pinheads", and dust thoroughly.

The surface is now ready for the background coat of paint, which is applied in the way which has been described for wood surfaces in Chapter 4.

Note on Painting Trays

If you are painting a tray, rest it upside down on the palm of your left hand, and apply paint to the underside of the flange. Do *not* paint the bottom, since that is left unpainted to provide a resting place while the tray is drying. Next, turn the tray over, so as to rest the unpainted bottom on your left palm, and continue the painting in this order: first the outer edge of the tray, then the top of the flange, and finally the floor of the tray. Use long strokes, the full length of the tray's floor.

Only when all the other work on the tray has been completed, including the finishing coats of varnish, and the last rubbing down, is the bottom of the tray given one or two coats of black paint, nothing more. Occasionally, collectors and dealers in antiques do not want the bottom of a tray touched by paint because many of them can judge age and condition by careful examination of the unpainted bottoms of trays.

6

How to Mix
Background Colors

How to apply a flat background paint to a surface has already been
described (Chapter 4), and here we shall deal with the mixing of colors
for that purpose.

Before making use of any of the colored backgrounds, however, the
beginner is advised to work for some time on a black background only.
Corrections are not so noticeable on black, and black was often used by
the old craftsmen.

Paints to Use

For background colors we generally use good-quality, flat indoor
paints. Never use glossy enamels. Pratt & Lambert's Sta Blac *Flat*
Enamel, among others, gives an excellent dull black surface when it is
sufficiently thinned with turpentine. Always remember to mix paint
thoroughly before using.

Most of our other background colors have to be obtained by mixing,
and for this work we can use small screw-top jars, such as cold-cream
jars. It is important when mixing a color to be sure there will be
enough left over for touching up after the decoration has been completed. The closed jars serve to keep the colors fresh.

In mixing for a background color, mix the pigments first, and then
add the turpentine to get the proper watery consistency. For this
reason, mix a relatively small quantity of the pigment color, allowing
for the fact that you will have a much larger quantity after the turpentine has been added.

Japan colors mixed with our artist's oil colors can be used for
background colors. But for large areas this is expensive, and so we
generally start with a can of flat paint nearest to the color we want,

[*32*]

adding tube colors to get the exact shade. Economy is also served by using for this purpose the less expensive tube oil colors, which can be procured in some of the larger paint stores.

Antique Black

To obtain antique black, put a little flat black in a clean jar, adding to it some Raw Umber and White. The best way to go about this is to squeeze a little of the two last-named pigments on to an old saucer, and to dissolve them by mixing in some of the black with a showcard brush or a palette knife. When no lumps remain, add the mixture to the jar of flat black, and stir well with a small stick. Test the color on a piece of paper, using the showcard brush. Keep mixing and adding until the proper shade has been reached. Antique black is really off-black, that is, a very dark, soft, charcoal color. It is very effective as a background for country patterns.

Brown

If the brown you buy needs to be modified it may be done by adding—

White to make it lighter,
Yellow to make it lighter and warmer,
A little Vermilion to make it lighter and still warmer,
Blue to make it darker and colder.

Light Colors

Use flat white paint as a base for all light colors, adding Japan or oil colors to get the desired color. Always allow for the darkening effect of the finishing coats of varnish and, of course, for any antiquing you may intend to do. Among the most used light background colors are these:

Off-White: White with a little Raw Umber added.
Cream: White with a little Yellow Ochre added.
Gray: White with a little Raw Umber added.
Tan: White with a little Burnt Umber added.

Medium Colors

Use the nearest available color in flat paint, and add the necessary tube colors as indicated below.

Antique Red: To get a lovely soft red, such as the background color

[*33*]

on the Foot Bath pattern in Color Plate IX, mix a flat red paint with Raw Umber, Chrome Yellow, and a little White. Avoid using Vermilion as it never mixes thoroughly with other pigments, making it almost impossible to get an even background color. Start with ordinary red, indoor, flat paint to reach the color you want.

Mustard Yellows: These are a group of beautiful colors, almost endless in their variations. The result depends on the kind of brown you add to yellow, whether it be Raw Umber, Burnt Umber, or Burnt Sienna, and also on the quantity of White you add, if any. The addition of Raw Umber to Chrome Yellow gives a greenish mustard color, varying with the amount added. Burnt Umber gives a warmer mustard, and Burnt Sienna a rich golden-orange mustard yellow.

Antique Blue: Blue was not used so much as the other colors in the old days, because blue was made from indigo which had be imported. A good antique blue can be made by mixing White and Raw Umber together, and then adding Prussian Blue. The latter is a powerful color, and a little of it goes a long way.

Asphaltum

A background which differs from the colors proper is "asphaltum," a mixture of asphaltum (or asphalt) and varnish. It is a semi-transparent background which was often used over bright tin, but it is difficult to apply satisfactorily. Old examples invariably show more or less streakiness, and therefore beginners need not be unduly discouraged by the results of their first attempts.

If the tin has darkened with age or use, no longer presenting a uniformly bright surface, apply a coat of clear varnish. When this is tacky, that is, not quite dry, apply aluminum or chrome powder with a piece of velvet, and then burnish it with the velvet. This will give a simulated shiny tin surface. After a wait of 24 hours, wash off all loose powder under running cold water, pat the surface thoroughly dry with a lintless cloth, and apply a coat of varnish to protect the surface. Let it dry for another 24 hours.

Asphaltum can be bought in a tube. It should be mixed in a saucer with varnish, to which is added a little each of Alizarin Crimson and of Burnt Umber. The quantity used of these oil colors determines the color of the asphaltum, and the quantity of varnish determines its transparency.

Apply the mixture with a varnish brush, working quickly. Do not go back and retouch any part of it. If you have enough of the mixture on your brush as you apply it, the streakiness may disappear when the asphaltum settles. Use discarded tin cans to experiment with in applying the mixture, and find out what shade of background you like best. Asphaltum must be allowed to dry for at least a week.

The coffee pot and sugar bowl in Color Plate V have asphaltum backgrounds.

7

How to Transfer a Design

When a freehand design is to be painted on a tray, chair, or other object, the design must be transferred to the painted surface of the object. To do this, a careful tracing of the design is made on tracing paper, including everything except the superimposed details, which can be added later by comparison with the original design. Use a well-sharpened H or 2H pencil to make the tracing.

In order to transfer the traced design to the object's surface, a form of carbon paper is necessary. Commercial carbon papers, being greasy, are quite unsuitable for this work. Consequently we make our own kinds of "carbon" papers, as described below, and keep them in hand for future use.

Homemade "Carbons"

A white "carbon" is required to transfer to dark backgrounds. Take a sheet of tracing paper, size about 6″ × 12″. Rub a cake of magnesium carbonate (see Chapter 2) over the surface; then rub the deposited powder well into the paper with your fingertips. Blow off the excess powder on the tracing paper. Fold the paper in half with the white powder on the inside of the fold. Put the folded paper under a book, or in a portfolio, so that some pressure is on it. Leave it there for a week, during which time the white powder will work into the surface of the tracing paper. A smaller white carbon, about 4″ × 8″, is desirable for smaller jobs.

A dark "carbon" for transfers to light or medium backgrounds is made by penciling a sheet of tracing paper with the flat side of the point of an H or 2H pencil. Do *not* use a soft smudgy pencil. This time there is no need to use the fingers, and the carbon paper thus made can be used immediately without any waiting period.

Transferring to a Dark Background

Place your pencil tracing of the design in position on the surface to be decorated, making sure the design is *exactly* where you want it to be. (Consider this point very carefully, not only looking at the tracing, but consulting also your finished copy of the pattern on frosted acetate. Once the design has been painted, if a careless placing shows up, it is often impossible to correct it without doing all the work over again).

Secure the tracing to the surface with 2 or 3 tiny pieces of masking tape, so placed that you can slide your white carbon paper, white side down, underneath the tracing without disturbing the tape.

Then proceed to retrace the design with a well-sharpened 3H pencil. Move the carbon along when and if necessary to keep it under the pencil point. When you have finished retracing, and have removed the tracing paper and carbon, you will find a white outline of the pattern left on the object. Then you proceed to paint the pattern as you did on your acetate copy.

Transferring to a Light Background

Proceed as for a dark background, using your pencil "carbon" paper instead of the white one.

8

How to Stripe

There are some old decorated pieces which have no stripes, but it is correct to say that most of them do include some striping. Nothing will help to give a "professional" touch to your work more than a well-executed bit of striping. It is most desirable, therefore, that you should learn how to paint a stripe.

At first, this may seem difficult, but the fact is that striping is easily learned, given a certain amount of practice. Practice steadies the hand, and you soon gain facility in the use of the brush.

The proper brush for striping is a square-tipped, camel's-hair, or badger hair, quill brush, with hairs about 1½ inches long, and about #1 in thickness. The brush is used without a handle, and in the act of striping, the brush is always pulled towards you. (See Plate 6).

Begin by half filling a bottle cap with varnish. Using a showcard brush, mix in with the varnish a little Japan Yellow and a touch of Burnt Umber, until the color is a fairly thin mustard yellow. With the brush, lift out some of the mixture on the newspaper palette. Dip the striper into the mixture on the palette, moderately loading it the full length of the hairs. Pull it back and forth on the newspaper to get the feel of the brush.

Practice striping first on a piece of paper, always pulling the striper towards you. The stripe should be about ⅛ inch wide. To get a narrower stripe, flatten the brush on the newspaper palette by pulling it back and forth a few times, and then stripe with the thin edge of the brush.

Some of the old chairs, trays, etc., have opaque stripes, while others have stripes which are semi-transparent. In the former instance, less varnish is used in the mixture in proportion to the paint; in the latter, more varnish.

[*38*]

The student may find it helpful to practice striping on a raw tray, and thus get the feel of working on an object. The paint can easily be cleaned off the tin with Carbona. With a striper adequately loaded with paint, you should be able to stripe one side of a tray without replenishing the brush.

In striping a rectangular shape, such as a chair slat, do not try to make two stripes meet in a perfect angle. Instead, carry the stripes across one another and on to the ends of the area. This done, *immediately* clean off the bits of striping outside the intersection by wiping with a clean cloth. Or touch up with background paint when dry.

Striping is best done on a glossy or varnished surface that is thoroughly dry. As will be described in the next chapter, after a decoration is completed, the object is given several finishing coats of varnish. Where there is striping, however, one such coat should be put on before the striping is done, and should be allowed to dry for 24 hours. After the striping, the finishing coats of varnish are applied. The glossy surface keeps the stripe from "fuzzing" at the edges, and also facilitates corrections. These adjustments must be done at once, if you use either a clean cloth or a cloth and a little Carbona to wipe away the surplus. Another, and often easier, way to make corrections is to wait until the stripe is thoroughly dry, and then to touch it up with the background paint. This, of course, means waiting until the next day.

For a very broad band or stripe, outline the stripe, and then fill it in.

9

The Final Stages

Varnishing

To protect a decorated object from wear and tear, and also to give it the satin smooth finish characteristic of an old piece, we apply at least six coats of varnish after the decoration has been completed. On trays and table tops (for which a heatproof and alcohol-resistant surface is always desirable) the last two coats should be of Super Valspar varnish, procurable in most paint stores.

Antiquing

Some of the coats of varnish may be toned with oil pigments to give an antique color, and this process we call antiquing. The varnish so tinted must remain completely transparent, and therefore only a very little color should be used. Otherwise unsightly streaks will appear on the decorated surface. For most purposes we use Burnt Umber or Raw Umber, but Indian Yellow, Black, or Prussian Blue are occasionally used. Antiquing is generally done with the first coat, or the first two or three coats, depending on the depth of color you want. Since most beginners tend to over-antique, it is a good thing to act on the principle that a little antiquing goes a long way.

Conditions Necessary for Varnishing

It is important to do all varnishing in an atmosphere free from dust. Clean the room first, and allow the dust to settle. Close the windows, and while the varnish is drying keep traffic away from the room for the first three or four hours.

Varnish should be applied in a warm room, one in which the temperature is 70 degrees or more. The varnish itself should be at least that warm, and so should the object to be varnished. To achieve this, let them both stand in the room for some time before the varnishing is

[*40*]

begun. They may be placed near a radiator to raise their temperature a little. Varnish applied to a cold surface or in a cold room will "crawl" —that is, will tend to separate, leaving bare places—and "ridge."

How to Proceed—First Day

Taking a tin tray as our example, we will now go step by step through the procedure of varnishing, antiquing, and the other processes of finishing.

Before you open the can of varnish, assemble the necessary equipment, which consists of plenty of newspapers, the varnish brush, paint rags, and the "brush bath," a jar half full of turpentine for cleaning the brush. Flick the dry brush to get rid of any lose hairs or dust particles.

Dust the tray carefully, and place it on clean newspapers. Decide where to put the tray to dry after it has been varnished, and spread newspapers there. Place a can or other firmly set stand on which the wet tray may finally be rested approximately in the center of the spread newspapers. Just before beginning to varnish, wipe the tray again, this time with the palm of your hand, so as to remove any remaining lint or dust particles, especially from the corners. Now you are ready.

On a clean newspaper palette squeeze out a little Burnt Umber. (We are assuming that antiquing is desired—if it is not, of course, you omit the Burnt Umber.) Using your one-inch varnish brush, dip out four or five brushfuls of varnish, and mix with them on the palette a touch of Burnt Umber. Try it out on a clean piece of paper to test the color, which should not be much darker than the clear varnish itself. Work quickly because varnish thickens on contact with the air.

If it is the right color—that is, a very pale brown—start to varnish the tray at once. Support the tray on the palm of your left hand. First do the underside of the flange, then the edge, then the top side of the flange, and finally the floor. (Refer back to the last paragraph of Chapter 5, where the method of holding a tray while painting it is described.) Don't flood the varnish on, as that will only cause the excess to run down and settle in the corners, where it cannot dry properly. Spread the varnish out, and work with the light falling across your work, so as to enable you to see that every bit of surface is being covered. Work quickly and surely, taking more varnish only as you need it, but never flooding the surface. Then, without taking any more varnish unless it is absolutely necessary, use the brush in a crosswise direction to ensure an even distribution. If it becomes necessary to mix more varnish and Burnt Umber as you work, do it as rapidly as possible, but keep a sharp watch lest any brown streaks appear; that would mean that you have added too much color to the varnish.

When everything is covered, examine the work, and with a very light touch, using only the tip of the brush, pick up any tiny bubbles or any brush hairs which may be on the surface. Last of all, hold the tray high, and pick up with the brush any varnish drippings from the underside. Set the tray down on the prepared stand, and leave it to dry for 24 hours.

Second Day

Dust off the tray, and apply the second coat of varnish, adding a touch of Burnt Umber if you want a darker color. Dry for 24 hours.

Third Day

Dust off, and apply the third coat of varnish. Dry for 24 hours.

Fourth Day

Cut some *very fine* sandpaper into 1½ by 3½ inch pieces, and fold them in half, with the sand outside. Sandpaper the surface with these small pieces. Starting on the floor of the tray, sandpaper diagonally, first from upper left to lower right, and next from upper right to lower left. Work on small sections in turn. When one hand is tired, use the other, and by thus changing back and forth you will save time and not become fatigued.

Although sandpapering has to be thorough, you must be careful not to do it too long or to press too hard, or you might go right through the coats of varnish. Once the floor of the tray has been sanded, do the flanges, keeping away from the edges, where the sandpaper can very easily take off both varnish and paint. Naturally, this caution must be observed in dealing with any kind of object, large or small.

After the sanding is completed, dust off the tray. If any sand particles are stuck in the corners, it shows you used too much varnish previously, with the result that it could not dry properly. In this event, you will have to wait another 24 hours for the varnish to dry, after which the corners may be sanded out.

Apply the fourth coat of varnish, and allow it to dry for 24 hours.

Fifth Day

Sandpaper the surface as described above. Dust off thoroughly. Apply a coat of Super Valspar varnish (in the case of trays and table tops, otherwise ordinary varnish again). This is a heavier varnish than the previous coats, so that you must work quickly and vigorously to brush it all over the surface before it starts to set. Let it dry for 24 hours.

Sixth Day

Instead of sandpaper, use steel wool #000, rubbing on the diagonal again. In dusting off, be sure to get all the remnants of steel wool out of the corners. Apply another coat of Super Valspar (or ordinary varnish where appropriate), and let it dry for 48 hours.

Final Rubbing

In an old saucer, place about a teaspoonful of powdered pumice. Take a soft cotton flannel cloth, and put a little crude oil on it. Dip the oiled cloth into the pumice, and begin to rub a small section of the tray, a few square inches at a time. There is no need to rub long, for the high gloss of the varnish comes off immediately. If you rub too much, you will give the tray a dull, lifeless finish, whereas the proper effect is that of a satiny gleam. This is achieved very quickly, and without strenuous effort. Use enough crude oil to keep the rubbing moist.

When you have gone over the whole tray, rub off the remains of the oil and pumice with a clean flannelette cloth, and let the surface dry. In about fifteen minutes inspect the surface, and if any bright glossy spots are visible, give them a rubbing as before. Wipe off again with a clean cloth. This satiny finish needs no furniture polish to preserve it. All it needs is the application now and then of a damp cloth.

PLATE I   FRAKTUR DESIGN FROM A BOOKPLATE
(courtesy of Pennsylvania German Society)

[*45*]

PLATE II FLOWER PAINTING
(courtesy of Pennsylvania German Society)

PLATE III   THREE MUSICIANS AND TULIP
(courtesy of Metropolitan Museum of Art)

PLATE IV HORIZONTAL MOTIFS
(courtesy of New York Historical Society)

10

How to Make Designs
Larger or Smaller

Enlarging or reducing a design is a simple, almost mechanical process, the successive steps of which are given below. We may conveniently take the small flower in Plate 3 to illustrate enlarging.

To Enlarge a Design

1. Trace the flower (or whatever else you may choose to enlarge) on the upper left-hand corner of a piece of tracing paper large enough to contain also the enlarged size you want.

2. Draw a rectangle around the flower which will just box it in and touch it on all four sides. Use a small right-angle triangle or a postcard to get right angles at all the corners. Draw with a well-sharpened 2H pencil.

3. Extend the right-hand side of the rectangle downwards several inches, and extend the bottom line several inches out to the right.

4. Using a ruler, draw a line diagonally from the upper left-hand corner to the lower right one and beyond, as in the illustration.

5. Measure either the width or the height of the larger size that you want, and complete the larger rectangle. Use the triangle or the postcard to get right angles at the corners, and be sure the diagonal already drawn passes through the lower right-hand corner. This ensures that the enlarged size will be in the same proportion as the original.

6. With the ruler, divide the sides of the smaller rectangle in half, then in quarters, and then in eighths. Do the same with the larger rectangle. If the design is more complicated than our present example, divide the sides into sixteenths or even thirty-seconds.

7. Rule in the lines and number them as shown in the illustration.

8. You will observe that the outline of the smaller flower is crossed by the dividing lines at certain points in the little square. Where these points occur, place a dot in the corresponding place in the larger square. Watch the numbers to be sure you are in the corresponding square each time. When all the dots are in, join them up with lines of the same character as those in the original.

9. If the finished flower looks a little stiff, put a fresh piece of tracing paper over it, and retrace it. While doing this you have an opportunity to improve the drawing.

To Reduce a Design

Proceed in the same way as for enlarging, but this time when extending the bottom and right-hand sides of the rectangle you will, of course, make a *smaller* rectangle, corresponding to the size of the reduction you need. (By turning Plate 3 upside down you can see how the two rectangles should look for reducing purposes.)

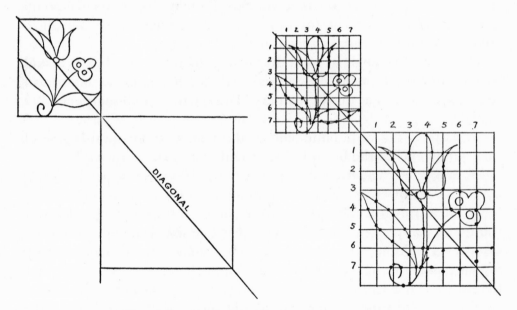

PLATE 3   ENLARGING AND REDUCING A DESIGN

[*50*]

11

How to Use and
Adapt Designs

If you are decorating objects which are reproductions of old pieces, it is particularly important to use appropriate designs. For example, use a wooden box design on a wooden box, and a country tin design on a piece of tinware. Make a habit of studying old pieces so that you will know what is appropriate.

If you are decorating modern pieces with these old folk patterns, I can think of no sound objection to allowing oneself a somewhat greater freedom in the choice of a design to be used. Good taste, however, must be our guiding principle.

You may be a trained artist and have thus taken some pains to cultivate good taste, but unless you are, it would be unsafe to assume that you were born with it ready-made. Few people are, but fortunately most people can develop it. So let us all be a little humble in this matter, and take every opportunity to improve our appreciation of decorative art. Visit museums to study the old pieces, noting how they were decorated, how much space was left around the designs, how the colors were combined, and so on. Take notes, and make little rough sketches as the professionals do. If no museums are handy, study old pieces in houses where you may visit, or in the windows of antique shops. In the latter case you may find it more discreet to make only mental notes on the spot.

In this book nothing has been said in the way of instruction in the restoring of painted decorations on old pieces, because this is a book chiefly for those who are starting to learn to decorate. At this stage no one should attempt restorations, but should wait until a good deal of experience has been acquired. Old pieces, of whatever nature, are valuable from more than one point of view, and we should not risk ruining them. If, however, you are an experienced decorator and want information on the restoration of old pieces, you may find it helpful to refer to the chapter on "Restoring Decorated Articles" in my earlier book, *American Antique Decoration.*

Naturally, there are times when we have to enlarge or reduce designs to fit the available space. But do not carry this to great extremes. Thus if you need a large design, do not enlarge a very small one, but choose one nearer in size to what you want.

If the proportions of a design need to be adapted, if for instance you want a design to be a little longer but not at the same time any wider, proceed as follows: First mark out on a sheet of tracing paper the area you want to fill. Put this tracing over the original pattern, and proceed to make a revised drawing of the pattern according to your needs. You move the tracing paper so that the different parts of the design will appear where you want them. When you are working in a larger area, you may find it desirable to enlarge or multiply some parts. For example, a central flower or fruit may be expanded in size, or two small leaves may be increased to three. Similarly for smaller areas, parts may be reduced or omitted altogether. Such changes are made by the eye, and judgment is used to preserve balance and good proportion in the whole design. Generally speaking, adaptations should aim at keeping an original design as little changed as possible.

In our resolution to exercise good taste, we include two "don'ts" which it should not be difficult to follow. One is, don't *over*-decorate by crowding in every possible thing. And the other is, of course, don't go to the opposite extreme and put some mousy little design on a huge piece of furniture!

12

Reverse Painting on Glass

Paintings on glass were used to adorn many of the old mirrors and clocks. These decorative paintings were done on the back of the glass panel in *reverse,* so that the correct picture or design was seen through the glass from the front. The detail was therefore painted first, and the sky or background last. Various subjects were used, including landscapes, buildings, seascapes, ships, fruits, flowers, figures, portraits, and formal designs; in fact, reverse paintings were made of almost any subject that might appeal to the craftsman's or his customer's fancy. Some of the paintings were crudely done; others reflect the skill of an experienced artist.

The glass pattern shown in line in Plate 4, and in color in Plate VI, was taken from the old mirror which can be seen in Plate D. Old glass paintings were done on very thin glass, so when you come to do one, use a piece of thin glass. But before that you should do a practice copy.

How to Copy a Pattern

To copy the pattern in Plate 4 follow the detailed steps given below. Of course, you will use a piece of frosted acetate for this preliminary practice.

1. Make a pencil tracing of the pattern on tracing paper. Put it face down on a white cardboard, and secure it at the corners with masking tape. This gives you the pattern in reverse. Note that the drawing in Plate 4 is given to you just as I traced it from the old mirror, and has *not* been reversed.

2. Place a piece of frosted acetate over your reversed tracing, and with pen and ink put in the black dots which outline the trees, houses, and fence. Paint the horizontal line which runs completely across under the buildings, fence, etc., in Burnt Umber. Also put in the black foreground using Lamp Black thinned well with varnish, so that it is transparent in places. This completes the first stage. Wait 24 hours.

3. Certain parts of the picture are done in *transparent* colors, and these are to be painted now. (Refer to p. 22 for the mixing of transparent colors). It is convenient to divide the work into two parts, (a) and (b).

(a) Mix some Prussian Blue and Indian Yellow to make a transparent bluish green, and apply this to all the diagonally shaded parts of the picture. Begin with one of the trees, using two or three strokes of the brush. Immediately take a clear varnish brush and blend the edges. Do the same with the next tree, and so on with the rest. Apply this same color to the windows and doors, but here the edges are not blended off as you can clearly see from the Color Plate VI. Some of the windows and doors appear to be done in a different color in the colored Plate, but this is only because there are other colors painted behind the dark green in the next stage of the work. Now apply this same green to the lawn, but of course only to the shaded part of it, and blend off the edges here and there. Leave for 24 hours.

(b) For the transparent color touches in the sky, you will need to work with three brushes. With one brush, mix Prussian Blue and a touch of Raw Umber to make a dark transparent blue. With the second brush, mix Burnt Umber and Yellow Ochre to make a transparent yellowish brown. In each case the mixture should consist mostly of varnish with just enough pigment to give the color you want. Try it out on the edge of the newspaper palette.

First, apply this blue to the wavy horizontal areas of the sky. Next, paint the fine dotted area of the sky with the yellowish brown. Immediately use the third brush, with just a little varnish on it, to blend the edges of the colors here and there.

To paint the dark red of the roofs and chimneys, shown crosshatched in the drawing, mix Alizarin Crimson and a little Burnt Umber to make a rich dark transparent red. Leave for 24 hours.

It is possible to do the work described under both (a) and (b) in one operation. However, it is easier to divide the work as suggested above.

4. At this stage, referring to the Color Plate VI for guidance, we apply the opaque colors on the buildings, fence, trees, and lawn. For the orange color on the smaller house, mix Japan Yellow, Japan Vermilion, and enough Burnt Umber to obtain a dull orange. Apply this to the side, roof, and chimney, going right over the green windows and the dark red roof and chimney. Pick up one edge of the acetate to see the effect on the "front" side. The same color goes over the other dark red parts.

The mustard yellow on the larger building is a mixture of Japan Yellow, Raw Umber, and a little White, and is applied right over the

BLUE

CREAM

DARK BLUE

PALER BLUE

PINK

BROWN LINE

CREAM

PALER BLUE

PINK

PINK

YELLOWISH BROWN

CREAM

PINK

PLATE 4 REVERSE PAINTING ON GLASS

windows and doors. For the white sections, mix White and a little Raw Umber to get an off-white. For the opaque green on the trees and lawn, mix Japan Green with Burnt Umber and a touch of Yellow Ochre. Let dry 24 hours.

5. The next stage is the completion of the sky. Some artists prefer to use regular flat artist's oil brushes (about ¼ inch wide for this work); others like the showcard brushes. The quill-brushes are too soft. Whatever brushes you use, you should have three of them, one each for the blue, the pale pink, and the cream color. Mix all three colors before you start to paint. Work quickly, because varnish thickens on contact with the air.

Mix White, Raw Umber, and a little Prussian Blue to get the blue of the sky at the top of the Color Plate VI. You can easily add a little more White when you paint the paler blue of the distant sky lower down in the picture. For the pale pink, mix White, Raw Umber, and a touch of Alizarin Crimson and of Yellow Ochre. For the cream color, mix White, Yellow Ochre, and a touch of Burnt Umber.

In painting the sky, don't do it by filling in spaces, but paint right across the picture, covering the buildings and trees. Keep watching the other side of the acetate to judge the effect. Some artists use their fingers to blend the edges where two colors meet. Dry the work for 48 hours.

6. Apply a coat of white paint over everything.

To Paint on Glass

To do this pattern on a piece of glass, first of all clean both sides of the glass with a piece of crumpled wet newspaper. Then take another piece of newspaper, dry this time, crumple it, and use it to dry the glass thoroughly. The important thing to remember is that the glass must be thoroughly clean. You may have other methods of cleaning glass which you feel are preferable.

Next, give one side of the glass a coat of varnish, antiqued with a little Raw Umber. Let it dry for 24 hours. See Chapter 9.

Finally, proceed to paint the pattern on the glass as you did previously on the acetate. You work on the varnished surface, which will not only enable you to use the pen and ink without difficulty, but will give an air of antiquity to the whole picture.

Framed Picture

If you wish to paint a glass to be used as a framed picture on the wall, it will save time and bother if you buy a glass to paint which already has a frame.

13

Designs from Old Fraktur Paintings

Fraktur paintings, described and discussed historically in Chapter 1, were usually done on white paper. The design was first outlined in brown* ink with a goose quill, and the colors, generally water-color dyes, were then applied with a brush, which often was a homemade cat's-hair brush. The photographs (pp. 25-26) show two fine examples of this class of work.

Many of the motifs found in Fraktur designs are so beautiful that they can stand alone simply as pictures for framing and hanging on the walls. Consider, for example, Color Plates I and II. Fraktur can also be used to provide decorative ideas in stenciling and silk screening on fabrics and stationery, in embroidery, in making appliqué quilts and in the decorating of furniture and smaller objects.

Since the originals were most often done on white paper, it would be best to use these motifs on light backgrounds, such as off-white or cream. The designs can first be outlined with a fine pen line in brown waterproof drawing ink, the transparent colors being then applied. If you find it difficult to get a good pen line on a painted surface, give the surface a coat of varnish first. Let it dry 24 hours, and then go over it lightly with steel wool, just sufficiently to take off the high gloss. This makes the surface more receptive to the ink and, moreover, makes it easier to carry out corrections with Carbona Cleaning Fluid.

If you are decorating wooden-ware or tinware, use artist's oil colors thinned with varnish for your transparent colors. If you prefer to use opaque colors, which are easier to apply, the motifs should *not* be outlined first in ink, but the flat opaque color applied. After that, it is not usually necessary to add an outline.

* The early illuminators had black, green, blue, red, and yellow inks. The black ink turned brown in the course of time, as ancient writing has done in documents everywhere. This is probably the reason why the later Pennsylvania scribes and decorators often used a brown ink which would imitate the effect of antique ink.

When doing a picture to be framed, use water-color paper, outline the motif in brown waterproof drawing ink, and then use water colors to fill in the design.

Whatever kinds of paint you use, be sure to add a little brown to all reds, greens, yellows, and blues to achieve soft but still bright antique colors. Guard against adding too much brown, for that will result in dull, sad colors; but garish crude colors are quite out of place in this work.

The figures in Plates 22 and 23 and Color Plate III were taken from an old Fraktur that was much faded, and in the reproduction some liberty has been taken with the colors, especially those on the three fiddlers. All these figures are typical of the Pennsylvania German spirit, which had great vitality and a keen zest for life. If the anatomical proportions are somewhat awry, nobody really minds, and the artist displays not only native vigor but great ingenuity in dealing with the somewhat difficult problem of drawing hands—he simply hides them. The hair in all the figures is left the color of the background, the details being inked in when the outlining is done. The hearts furnish a convenient place for initials and a date.

Pennsylvania German Fraktur birds make a wonderful collection. Several are shown in Plate 33. Such bird motifs were great favorites with the old artists, and they generally succeeded in depicting such wise and thoughtful-looking old birds.

Flower motifs appeal to all decorators, and some from Fraktur paintings are shown in Color Plate IV.

Beginners Should Wait

At this point I want to advise the beginner to postpone painting the tempting Fraktur patterns until all or at least the majority of the other patterns in this book have been painted on acetate. This is because these Fraktur patterns demand more skillful and finer drawing with the brush than do most of the other patterns. Naturally, much practice is neeedd to acquire the necessary facility.

The instructions given below for the more advanced student are kept brief, matters which will readily suggest themselves being omitted. We assume that you are using Japan and oil colors mixed with varnish.

Color Plate I (p. 45)

Mix some Japan Yellow with Burnt Umber and Burnt Sienna to make a warm golden mustard, and paint the over-all areas of the three flowers and the bowl. Wait 24 hours. With a medium country green, paint the leaves and the green bands on the bowl. Wait 24 hours. With an antique red, paint all the red parts. Add the black dots on the bowl, and the black accents on the leaves.

Color Plate II (p. 46)

Paint the mustard yellow parts first, then the red, then the green, and lastly the black.

Color Plate III (p. 47)

Musicians: Paint first the red, then the green, the mustard yellow, and the black in that order. Finally add the details on the coats.

Flower design: Paint the green first, then the red, the mustard yellow, and the black in that order.

Color Plate IV (p. 48)

Paint first the mustard yellow parts, then the red, the green, and the black in that order.

Plate 33

A. Mix Burnt Sienna with a touch of White, and paint the parts marked BS. With a dark country green, paint the parts shown in solid black. Wait 24 hours. With Japan Vermilion, paint the shaded areas. Wait 24 hours. Add the details on the birds in fine Black strokes. Eyes are Black.

B. Paint the leaves in light country green, and the shaded parts in Vermilion. With mustard yellow, paint the dotted parts. Wait 24 hours. With a dark country green, paint the areas shown in black. Wait 24 hours. Detail on bird's wing is in Black.

C and D. Paint the Vermilion first, then the mustard yellow. Wait 24 hours. Next, paint the Black. Outline the wings in Black.

Using Watercolor

If you want to paint one of these designs in watercolor on watercolor paper, you will naturally do the outlines first with a pen and brown waterproof drawing ink; then paint the black areas in black waterproof ink with a small pointed watercolor brush. Wait several hours to give the black ink time to harden. Then paint the colors, using the watercolor brush.

14

Decorated Barns

Besides their Fraktur paintings, the Pennsylvania Germans have given us another charming form of folk art in the decorated barn. The traveler through parts of Pennsylvania, chiefly Lebanon, Berks, Montgomery, and Lehigh counties, is delighted by the big, vividly colored geometric designs he sees painted on the barns. Some people call them "hex signs," and think they were originally intended to scare away demons and witches. One may surmise that "hex" is an abbreviation of hexagon, or of some kindred word, since six (Greek *hex*) points or angles are frequent in the designs. Similar designs were used on the walls, stained glass windows, and tessellated floors or pavements of churches and other buildings of medieval Europe. Although their religious or mystical significance may have been forgotten, it is not improbable that the farmers here did use them originally as protective devices. In any case, they applied them in a way as unique in this country as it is attractive.

The sketch on p. 74 represents one of the decorated barns. Dark red was commonly used for the background color, and the generally simple structural lines of the barns were often relieved by painting on the surface white columns and arches, in addition to the large circular geometric or "hex" designs. Plates 21 and 22 show the patterns of a few barn signs, and the colors used for them. But here we can show them only in miniature, for the originals are usually four to six feet in diameter! A string and a piece of chalk are the simple means used to draw the giant circles. Backgrounds less frequently seen than dark red are Yellow and dark olive-green.

15

Hints on Learning and Working

Anyone learning a new skill needs and should receive all the guidance and encouragement which the teacher can give. And this covers not merely the do's and don'ts of the technical instruction, but also whatever help of a more general kind the teacher's experience suggests will lead the student to success. So here are a few hints which have been useful to me and others.

1. You may find it helpful to read directions aloud to yourself a few times. Seeing an idea in print and at the same time hearing it spoken (by yourself in this case) are often more effective than the seeing alone.

2. To succeed in learning any skilled craft, you need practice, of course. But even more important, you must keep in your mind's eye a picture of yourself as doing beautifully whatever you seek to do. Concentrate only on success!

3. Get into the habit of following directions exactly. All directions have been worded so as to make them as plain and easy to follow as possible. If, in trying to carry out an operation new to you, something goes wrong, read every word of the instructions again. You'll probably find you missed some important point.

4. Nothing worth while in this world is accomplished without some thought. So think a process out before you act.

5. Don't try to rush the learning process. An idea new to you must have time to become a part of you. If nature takes many months to produce a flower, why should you expect to produce perfect brush strokes in one week?

6. There is only one way to get a job done—to get busy and do it. If your available time is limited to one hour, then do what you can in that hour.

7. It is important to keep your brushes, paints, varnish, all your equipment, in perfect condition at all times. Also keep your supplies and tools arranged in an orderly and convenient manner, so that you always know where each thing is.

8. Your acetate copies of patterns should each be mounted on cardboard or heavy paper with a wax-paper flap to protect them, and all should be kept together in filing folders or portfolios. They are the fruits of your time and labor, and time and labor are valuable. A portfolio can be made by folding a large sheet of plain or corrugated cardboard in half. Keep the larger patterns by themselves in a portfolio of their size.

9. Just a reminder of the value of acquiring the habit of studying old pieces, as advised in Chapter 11.

MORE PATTERNS

In describing the patterns which follow it won't be necessary to repeat instructions which you can find by referring to the chapters describing the main processes.

It is advisable to copy each pattern first on frosted acetate, so as to get the necessary practice in mixing colors and in painting the various stages. The beginner is also advised to spend five or ten minutes each day in practicing brush strokes, such as those shown in Plate 1, before going on to paint patterns. It saves time in the end because it makes for better work. You shouldn't be too easily satisfied with what you do. Aim at perfect brush strokes. Plate 1 can be a continually useful guide for practice work.

Blue Box

Line Plate 5 — Color Plate X (p. 68)

1. Look closely at the Color Plate X, and you will notice that the three large flowers have dark center areas. In Plate 5 these areas are enclosed by broken lines. Mix some Raw Umber and a little Lamp Black with enough varnish to make a semi-transparent dark gray, and apply this to a flower center, immediately blending off the edges with a clear varnish brush before going on to the next flower.

Mix Japan Green, a little Raw Umber, and a touch of White to make a country green, and paint all the leaves, stems, etc. Let it dry for 24 hours.

2. With a thin, semi-transparent, off-white mixture, paint the center rose and the date at the top.

With Japan Vermilion to which has been added a little Burnt Umber, paint all the solid black parts on Plate 5, disregarding the superimposed details. Wait 24 hours.

3. With a thin, transparent mixture of Japan Vermilion, apply the pale pink on the white rose, as indicated by the shaded parts on Plate 5. Add a bit more Vermilion to the mixture, and paint the darker accents on the lower petals. Add the red touches on the date.

With a thin, transparent mixture of Japan Black, add the dark overtones on the green leaves and stems, and on the red bow-knot, as shown by the crosshatched areas on Plate 5. Here and there, blend off *some* of the edges, to soften the general effect a bit. Wait 24 hours.

4. With a thin, semi-transparent off-white, add the center dots and white accents to the three small flowers; also the white highlights on the leaves and stems, and on the red bow-knot, where it is indicated by dotted areas (white dots being used on the black). Add a little Japan Yellow and Raw Umber to the brush, and apply the thin yellow touch on the lower part of the stem, as shown in the color Plate. Allow 24 hours for drying.

The blue background color for this pattern is made by mixing Prussian Blue, Raw Umber, a little White, and a touch of Alizarin Crimson.

[*63*]

XXXX TRANSPARENT BLACK
///// TRANSPARENT PINK
THIN OFF-WHITE
VERMILION

PLATE 5 BLUE BOX

PLATE V COFFEE POT AND SUGAR BOWL
(courtesy of Mrs. John Wood)

PLATE VI   REVERSE PAINTING ON GLASS

PLATE VII   ROSE CHAIR

PLATE VIII   WOODEN URNS

PLATE IX   PATTERNS FROM TINWARE

PLATE X   TWO WOODEN BOX PATTERNS

PLATE XI   PENNSYLVANIA GERMAN PATTERNS

Coffin Tray

Line Plate 6 — Color Plate IX (p. 67)

Small octagonal tin trays were made in considerable quantities during the 19th century by the local tinsmiths and received their quaint name because they were fashioned in a shape something like the old-style coffins. They were usually painted in black or asphaltum, but the brightly colored design was often painted on an off-white border. The pattern illustrated is a typical one. To decorate a tray with it, proceed as follows:

1. Paint your tray flat black in the usual way.

2. The off-white border on the floor of the tray starts right at the point where the floor or flat part of the tray meets the sloping flange. On a piece of tracing paper, trace the floor area of your tray, and then draw a second line 1⁵⁄₁₆ inches inward from that, thus creating the border area. Carefully measure with a ruler on each side to be sure the width of the border is the same all round. Transfer this second line to the tray, and paint in the off-white border, using a thin paint mixture to insure a smooth surface. Let it dry thoroughly.

3. Put your tracing back on to Plate 6, and trace the border motifs, disregarding all details which can be painted in later by eye. If your tray is a different size or shape, you may have to alter the size and positions of some of the motifs to suit it; but keep the red tomatoes in the middle of the long sides, and also keep the large leaves on either side of the tomatoes. Make any necessary changes at the corners and ends. Transfer the outlines of the design to the white border on the tray.

4. With Japan Vermilion paint all the areas marked V in Plate 6, disregarding all the superimposed details. Paint all the leaves marked with crosshatching in country green. With a rather thin mixture of Burnt Sienna and Burnt Umber, paint the large leaves and the smaller areas marked BS. Let the work dry for 24 hours.

5. Mix Japan Yellow and a little Raw Umber to make a mustard yellow, and paint the areas marked Y; also the dots which are represented by tiny *open* circles on the red grapes at the corners. Apply this

[*69*]

FLANGE OF TRAY

V   VERMILION
BS   BURNT SIENNA
▨▨▨   COUNTRY GREEN
Y   MUSTARD YELLOW
MB   MEDIUM BLUE
////// DARK TRANSPARENT RED
▦▦▦   THIN MUSTARD YELLOW

PLATE 6   COFFIN TRAY AND STRIPING

yellow to the dotted area on the tomatoes, immediately using a clear varnish brush to blend off the inner edge in each case.

With a medium blue, paint the parts marked MB.

With semi-transparent dark red, paint the shaded areas on the tomatoes and large flowers, immediately blending off the edges with a clear varnish brush as you paint each unit. Dry for 24 hours.

6. With Lamp Black, paint all the black accents, veins, stems, "whiskers," curlicues, dots, etc., shown in Plate 6.

7. Striping is in mustard yellow.

8. Finish the tray in the usual way.

New York Tin Box

Line Plates 7 and 8

Black is the background color of this old box, now in the Cooper Union Museum, New York. To copy the patterns (note that the end of the box is in Plate 8), proceed thus:

1. Paint the flowers and buds in salmon pink.

With a mixture of country green paint all the black areas. Let the work dry for 24 hours.

2. Paint the shaded strokes on the flowers and buds in semi-transparent dark red. Wait 24 hours.

3. With a semi-transparent off-white, paint the dotted strokes on the flowers and buds, and the large center vein on the leaves.

Mix some Japan Yellow and Raw Umber to make a mustard yellow; with this, paint all the remaining leaf strokes, stems, etc. Add more varnish to the mustard yellow to get a semi-transparent mixture, and paint the smaller side veins on the large leaves as shown by the white dotted lines. Wait 24 hours.

The brush strokes on the box top, the borders, and the striping are in mustard yellow. Also in mustard yellow is the crosshatching of the end design.

4. Finish the box in the usual way.

S   SALMON PINK

DARK TRANSPARENT RED

THIN OFF-WHITE

COUNTRY GREEN

Y   MUSTARD YELLOW

PLATE 7   NEW YORK TIN BOX

S   SALMON PINK
DARK TRANSPARENT RED
THIN OFF-WHITE
COUNTRY GREEN
Y   MUSTARD YELLOW

       PLATE 8 PENNSYLVANIA BARN AND END OF NEW YORK TIN BOX

Connecticut Chest

Line Plates 9, 10, 11, 12 — Photograph on p. 5

This pattern is from a blanket chest, which probably originated in Guildford, Connecticut, and is now in the Metropolitan Museum in New York. Made of oak and pine, it opens from the top and has one drawer at the bottom. It is dated 1705. This fine design is now much worn, but it is easy to see that when the chest was new it was a very attractive item indeed. The background color is dark oak.

On a sheet of tracing paper, make a complete tracing of the outlines of the thistle pattern, which is shown divided in Plates 9 and 12. Ignore the superimposed details. Mount the tracing on white cardboard, which will make the lines more easily seen, and fix a sheet of frosted acetate over it. Similarly make a tracing of the pattern in Plate 10, and its separated piece in Plate 12. Finally, make a tracing of the drawer pattern, the two parts of which are in Plates 11 and 12.

1. To paint the thistle motif in Plate 9, proceed as follows:

(a) The areas shown in white are all painted in a deep cream color, made by mixing White, Yellow Ochre, and a little Raw Umber. Paint the over-all area of the thistle, disregarding the heavy black crosshatching, the shaded dots, and the fine and heavy lines; similarly paint the over-all areas of the large leaves, the stems, small white leaves, and the base; also the over-all areas of the medium-sized and small flowers. Let the work dry for 24 hours.

(b) With Japan Black paint all the parts shown in heavy black, including the *heavier* black lines in the upper part of the thistle (not the thin ones). Mix Japan Green with a little Raw Umber to make a country green, and paint the small shaded leaves and the widely spaced "tartan" crosshatching on the two middle flowers. Let dry for 24 hours.

(c) With Japan Vermilion paint the large shaded dots on the lower part of the thistle, and on the small flowers; also the thin pen lines shown on the upper part of the thistle, on the large leaves, and on the central part of the two middle flowers. Let dry for 24 hours.

[75]

C   DARK CREAM
       COUNTRY GREEN
       VERMILION
       BLACK

CUT-OFF
SECTION
ON PLATE

PLATE 9   CONNECTICUT CHEST (a)

C   DEEP CREAM
///// VERMILION
■■ BLACK
∙.∙. DEEP CREAM DOTS

EL
1705.

CUT-OFF
SECTION
ON PLATE 12

PLATE 10   CONNECTICUT CHEST (b)   [77]

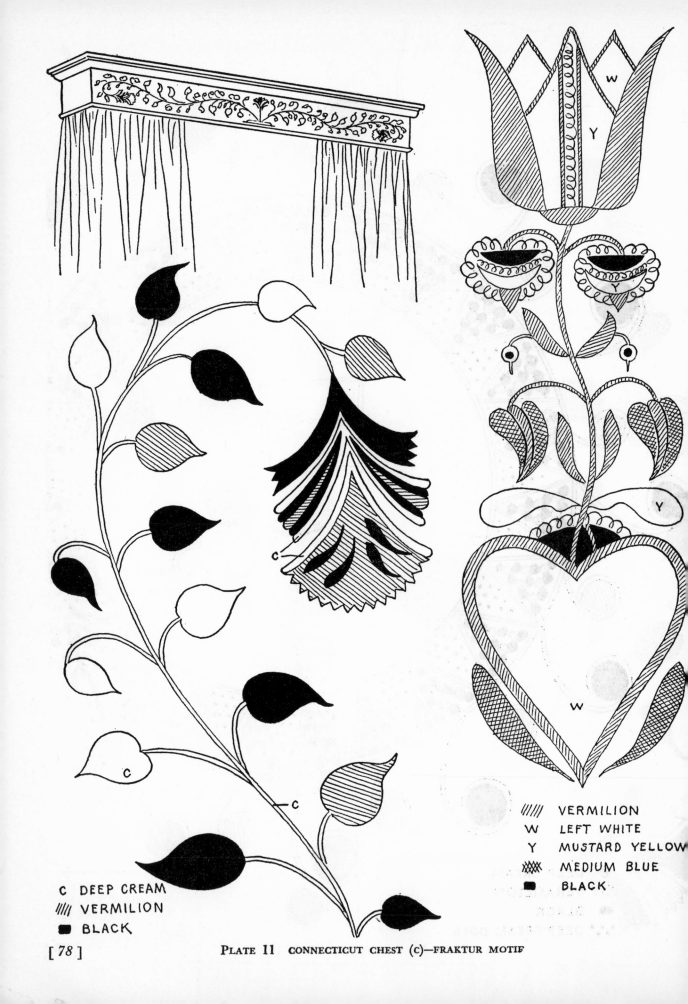

W   LEFT WHITE

Y   MUSTARD YELLOW

///// VERMILION

XXXX MEDIUM BLUE

■   BLACK

C   DEEP CREAM

///// VERMILION

■   BLACK

PLATE 11   CONNECTICUT CHEST (C)—FRAKTUR MOTIF

HANDLE

SEE PLATE 10

SEE PLATE 9

C

C

C

PLATE 12 CONNECTICUT CHEST (d)

2. For the pattern in Plate 10 the stages are:

(a) With the cream color used for Plate 9, paint the initials and date; then the two fine-line circles which outline the wide band; then the fine strokes marking off the little triangles inside the band. Use a striping brush for the two circles. Also in cream color are the very small pinpoint dots in the alternate triangles, and the swirling lines outside the band. Allow 24 hours for drying.

(b) Paint the large shaded dots and the shaded balls in Vermilion, and allow to dry for 24 hours.

(c) Paint the large black dots and the black balls in black.

In transferring this pattern to a surface that you want to decorate, there is no need to trace the dots within the wide band. Do these by eye. Be sure not to have an excess of paint on your brush, or the dots will spread after a few minutes and run into each other. The two large circles may be drawn with a compass.

Plates 11 and 12, which give half of the design on the drawer of the chest, are painted in a similar manner to the parts described above. The fine pen line veins on the leaf in Plate 12 are done in Vermilion. This design could be easily adapted for use on a cornice, as suggested by the sketch in Plate 11.

Pennsylvania German
Dough Trough

Line Plate 13

This pattern was taken from a Dauphin County, Pennsylvania dough trough which is preserved in the Metropolitan Museum of Art in New York. The utensil was made of poplar wood about the period 1780 to 1800. The two painted panels have a cream-colored background, while the over-all color of the trough is a deep honey.

1. Paint first the shaded areas in a mustard yellow, made by mixing Japan Yellow with Burnt Sienna. Then do the crosshatched areas in dark country green, made by mixing Japan Green with a little Raw Umber. Wait 24 hours.

2. The dotted areas are done in red, made by mixing Japan Vermilion with Yellow Ochre and a touch of Burnt Umber. The parts left plain white are to be painted in a dark blue. Allow 24 hours for drying.

3. The pot is done in an antique black, and so are the veins on the dark green, and the markings on the dark blue areas. Add more varnish to the antique black to make a semi-transparent black, and paint the markings on the red and yellow parts of the flowers.

For a deep honey color for the rest of the trough (or whatever you decorate), mix Japan Yellow, Burnt Umber, and White.

MUSTARD YELLOW
COUNTRY GREEN
VERMILION
D.B. DARK BLUE
BLACK

DB.

Tulip Box Pattern

Line Plate 14 — Color Plate XI (p. 68)

This pattern was taken from a Pennsylvania German wooden box dated 1763. The box was painted a creamy off-white, which is made by mixing White, Raw Umber, and Yellow Ochre. To copy this pattern on frosted acetate, the steps are:

1. On tracing paper make a complete tracing of the pattern shown in Plate 14. Mount this on white cardboard, so that the lines can be seen easily, and put a piece of frosted acetate over it.

2. With Japan Vermilion paint the over-all areas of the large tulip, the medium-sized flower on the left, and the fruit on the right. With a mixture of dark country green, paint all the leaves, stems, etc., as shown by the shaded areas in Plate 14, disregarding all the superimposed black and other details. Let the work dry for 24 hours.

3. With a mixture of mustard yellow, paint the areas marked Y on the large tulip, the center of the medium-sized flower, the single brush stroke on the fruit, and the small bell-like flowers on either side. Refer to the Color Plate XI for guidance all the time. Allow 24 hours for drying.

4. With Lamp Black, paint all the heavier black accents, brush strokes, and other detail shown in Plate 14. Wait 24 hours.

5. With a semi-transparent off-white, paint all the dotted brush strokes.

Suggested objects to which this pattern might be applied as a decoration include a chair, a window box, a chest of drawers, and a bread box.

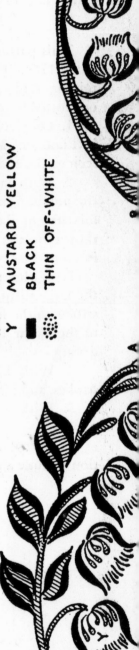

V VERMILION

DARK COUNTRY GREEN

Y MUSTARD YELLOW

BLACK

THIN OFF-WHITE

SKETCH A   GROUP OF OLD BOXES AND COUNTRY TINWARE

SKETCH B GROUP OF DECORATED FURNITURE

Sketch C   group of decorated small articles

Sketch D group of decorated small articles

Pennsylvania German
Foot Bath

Line Plates 15, 16, 17 — Color Plate IX (p. 67)

The background color on the old foot bath was a lovely soft antique red. To mix this color, see Chapter 6. In making a practice copy of the pattern on frosted acetate, your background can be a sheet of red paper, or you may paint a piece of cardboard red for the purpose. Then proceed in this order:

1. On a sheet of tracing paper of adequate size make a complete tracing of the outlines of the pattern from Plates 15, 16, and 17, ignoring all superimposed details. Mount this tracing on white cardboard, which will make the lines more easily seen, and fix a sheet of frosted acetate over it.

2. Looking at the Color Plate IX, you will notice that the three large fruits have dark shaded areas (indicated by line shading in Plates 16 and 17). These are actually the red background showing through a very thin mustard yellow. To paint these fruits, work with two brushes. On one brush have an ordinary mixture of mustard yellow, made by mixing Japan Yellow with Raw Umber. On the other brush have an extremely thin mixture that is mostly varnish with just a trace of the mustard yellow in it.

Do one fruit at a time, blending the thinner and heavier yellows where they meet. Work *quickly* to get the blending done before the varnish thickens. From time to time, slip the red paper under your painted fruits to see if you are getting the right effect.

With the heavier mustard yellow mixture, paint the rest of the yellow parts of the pattern, with the exception of the curlicues, which should be left to the very end when everything else on the pattern has been painted. Let dry 24 hours.

3. Mix some Japan Green, Raw Umber, a little Japan Yellow and a little White to get a soft country green, and paint all the green leaves, using the Color Plate IX as a guide.

Mix some White, Raw Umber, and a little Prussian Blue to get a rather light blue, and paint the light blue, crescent-shaped areas which surround the fruit marked F in the line illustration. The shading will be added later. Also paint all the round and oval grapes except those marked X, which are a light violet. Add a little Alizarin Crimson to your blue mixture to get a light violet, and paint the remaining grapes. In painting the grapes, disregard all the light and dark overtones and the black accents. Wait 24 hours.

4. With a thin mixture of Burnt Umber, apply the transparent brown overtones on the green leaves, as indicated by the shaded areas in the line illustration. Do one leaf at a time, and immediately blend off the inner edge of the brown, using a clear varnish brush.

If the darker parts of the three large fruits are not dark enough, an overtone of brown blended off at the edges will rectify this. Also, add the transparent brown shading on all the grapes, and on the light blue parts surrounding the fruit marked F, as indicated by the line shading in the illustration. Wait 24 hours.

5. With a semi-transparent mixture of off-white, paint the white strokes on the grapes, as indicated by the dotted areas in Plates 15, 16, and 17. Wait 24 hours.

6. With Lamp Black, paint all the black stems, veins, brush strokes, dots, accents, etc. Wait 24 hours.

7. With a mixture of mustard yellow, paint the tendrils or curlicues. Add some more varnish to the yellow to make a semi-transparent mustard yellow, and paint the highlights on the leaves. Add a little Japan Yellow to the mixture to make a brighter yellow, and paint the highlights on some of the yellow brush strokes, as indicated by the dotted outlines in the line illustration. Add the bright yellow dots on the fruit. This completes the pattern.

Striping on the foot bath was in mustard yellow.

PLATE 15 PENNSYLVANIA GERMAN FOOT BATH (a)

PLATE 16 PENNSYLVANIA GERMAN FOOT BATH (b)

PLATE 17   PENNSYLVANIA GERMAN FOOT BATH (C)

Cornucopia Canister

Line Plates 18 and 19 — Color Plate IX (p. 67)

To make a copy of this pattern on frosted acetate, proceed as follows:

1. On tracing paper make a complete tracing of the pattern from the drawing in Plate 18, and its continuation in the upper corner of Plate 19. Mount this on white cardboard, so that the lines can be seen easily, and put a sheet of frosted acetate over it.

2. With Japan Vermilion, paint the two large flowers, the buds, and the stems, *completely disregarding* at this time the black leaves which pass over the stems. Similarly paint the over-all shape of the cornucopia and the small buds around its edge, ignoring all the superimposed detail. Allow 24 hours for drying.

3. Now paint all the solid black parts of the illustration with a country green mixture, so thin that the red stems will just show through it, as well as a hint of the red cornucopia.

Mix some Alizarin Crimson and Burnt Umber to form a transparent dark red, and paint all the shaded brush strokes. Let it dry for 24 hours.

4. With a semi-transparent mixture of off-white, paint the dotted brush strokes.

With a mustard yellow made of Japan Yellow and Raw Umber, paint the lines forming the crosshatching on all the flowers; also the dots and stems on the cornucopia, and the hairline strokes projecting from its edge. With a semi-transparent mixture of the same yellow, paint the veins and highlight strokes which are indicated by broken white lines on the black leaves of the illustration.

Striping and borders are in mustard yellow. The brush stroke unit in the upper right-hand corner of Plate 1 would be appropriate on the cover of the canister. The background color of the canister (owned by Mrs. John G. McTernan, of Brooklyn, N.Y.) was black.

[*94*]

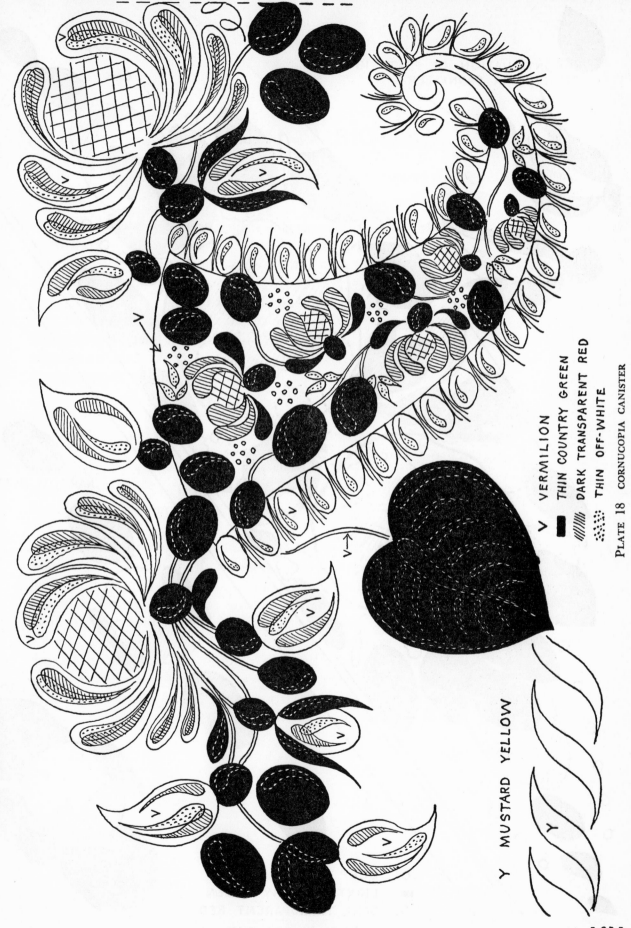

Y MUSTARD YELLOW

> VERMILION

▬ THIN COUNTRY GREEN

//// DARK TRANSPARENT RED

∴∴ THIN OFF-WHITE

PLATE 18 CORNUCOPIA CANISTER

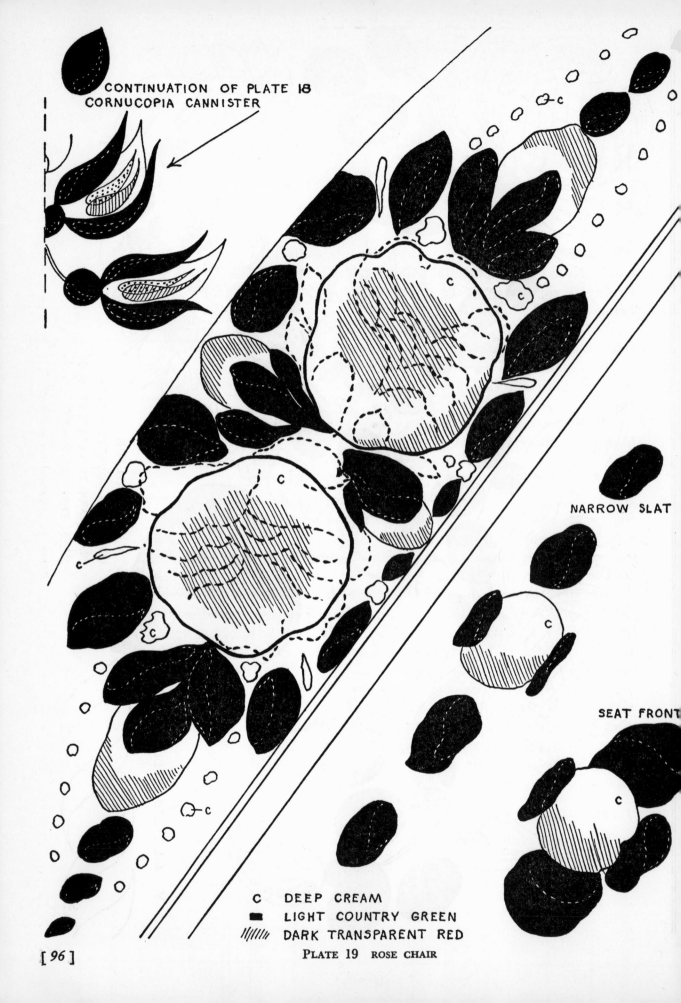

CONTINUATION OF PLATE 18
CORNUCOPIA CANNISTER

NARROW SLAT

SEAT FRONT

C   DEEP CREAM
■   LIGHT COUNTRY GREEN
///// DARK TRANSPARENT RED

PLATE 19 ROSE CHAIR

Rose Chair

Line Plate 19 — Color Plate VII (p. 66)

The steps for making a frosted acetate copy of the pattern in Plate 19 will be given first, and then the actual work on a chair will be described. (Disregard the design in the upper left-hand corner of Plate 19, that being a continuation of the previous Plate.)

1. Mix White, Raw Umber, and Yellow Ochre to get a deep cream color, and paint the over-all areas of the two roses, as shown by the heavy outlines. Disregard the shaded areas and the petal indications. Also paint the buds, and the uneven dots and strokes, all shown in white in Plate 19.

With a mixture of light country green, paint all the parts shown in black in the illustration. Wait 24 hours.

2. Mix Alizarin Crimson and Burnt Umber to form a transparent dark red; with this paint the shaded areas on the flowers and buds, one area at a time, and, *immediately* after each area is done, blend off the edges with a clear varnish brush before going on to the next shaded area. Work quickly, using as few strokes as possible, and with enough dark red on your brush for it to settle in a few minutes to form a smooth even color.

Mix some Prussian Blue and Indian Yellow to make a dark transparent green, and apply this to the areas indicated by the dotted white lines. Do one leaf at a time, blending off the inner edge of the dark green with a clear varnish brush before going on to the next leaf. Let the work dry for 24 hours.

3. Now the edges of the petals can be "veiled." Using hardly any varnish at all, mix a little White with a touch of Raw Umber to get a thick off-white with which to indicate the edges of the petals; this is known as "veiling." Paint one petal at a time, immediately taking a second brush with a little varnish on it to blend and soften the inner edge of each white stroke.

To Decorate a Chair

Before proceeding to decorate a chair with this pattern, you should

[*97*]

study the instructions on preparation of wood and on mixing background colors in Chapters 4 and 6. The background color for this chair is a dark reddish brown.

After the last coat of brown has been applied, allow it to harden for at least a week or two. Then refer to the Color Plate VII. There you will observe that gold bands have been applied around these parts: the side posts of the back just below the middle slat; the middles of the little spokes in the back; the front legs; and the front rung. These broad gold bands, found on many old chairs, were naturally varied according to the construction of the piece. Generally they adorned the round turnings. If your chair has no turned parts, you may suggest them by putting the gold bands where you think they would look well, as was done with the side posts of the back of the chair in the Color Plate.

The gold bands are applied before any of the painted decorations. For this work you will need some pale gold bronze lining powder, obtainable from an artist's supply store, and a small piece of satin-backed velvet ribbon, size about 2″ × 3″.

On a newspaper palette, and using a showcard brush, mix some varnish with a little Japan Vermilion to make a thin, semi-transparent red. With a few broad strokes of the brush, apply this mixture to the places chosen for the gold bands. Apply the paint evenly, so that no place is over wet. Do not go back and repaint any part—paint it and leave it. A flat, even surface is your objective. As you advance in the work, keep a watch on the bands already painted, and, as they begin to dry, apply pale gold powder to the tacky surface with the piece of velvet. Apply the powder with a very light touch, using a small circular motion. Continue in this way, painting and applying the powder to the drying bands. This method will give you a bright, shining gold effect.

The secret of success in this work is to apply the powder at just the right stage of dryness. If you do it too soon, the surface of the paint will be roughened, and some of the hairs of the velvet will stick to it. If you wait too long, the surface will be too dry for the powder to stick. The proper time varies from twenty minutes to an hour, according to the amount of varnish in your mixture, and according to the temperature and the moisture in the air. So it would be a good plan to get experience by painting a few patches on a piece of acetate, and experimenting in applying the powder to them before dealing with the chair.

When you have finished applying the last of the gold powder, let the chair dry for 24 hours.

Next day, gently wipe off all excess gold powder with a damp sponge, after which the surface may be dried by patting it with a linen towel. If powder still remains where it is not wanted, it can be painted out with the original background paint.

(As an historical note, the foregoing method of painting the gold bands was not the only one used in the old days, and you may find bands merely painted on a chair with a mixture of gold powder and varnish).

To paint the decoration, lay the chair on its back on your work table, and work upside down. Turn your pattern upside down, too, when you copy from it.

For the striping, refer to the Color Plate VII and decide how best to do your striping, taking into account the construction of your chair. The broad green stripe goes on first and is a mixture of Japan Green, Raw Umber, and a little White, using enough Raw Umber to get a dull green. The fine yellow stripe is a dull mustard, made by mixing Japan Yellow, Raw Umber, and a touch of White, and is applied when the green stripe is thoroughly dry.

Finish the chair in the usual way (see Chapter 9).

The original chair described in this chapter is owned by Mr. and Mrs. Vernon H. Brown of New York City.

YELLOW
BLUE GREEN
ORANGE RED

SIDE OF BOX

COUNTRY GREEN

BLACK
VERMILION

MUSTARD YELLOW

PLATE 21 TRINKET BOX (b) AND BARN SIGNS

Trinket Box

Line Plates 20 and 21 (part) — Color Plate XI (p. 68)

This pattern was taken from a Pennsylvania German trinket box, dating from about 1780. It is now in the museum of the New-York Historical Society. Plate 20 shows most of the top, the rest being continued on part of Plate 21, where also one of the sides of the box is shown. Referring to the Color Plate XI, you will see that the background is an antique black. The colors are all transparent ones, done over an off-white underpainting. Good practice may be obtained by first making a copy of the pattern on frosted acetate.

1. On a sheet of tracing paper, make a complete tracing of the pattern outlines from Plates 20 and 21, disregarding the shaded, crosshatched, and dotted indications of color. Mount this on gray cardboard, so that the lines can be seen easily, and put a sheet of frosted acetate over it.

2. With a mixture of off-white, paint the whole design, referring to the Color Plate XI for guidance. Allow 24 hours for drying.

3. With a mixture of transparent yellow (Indian Yellow or Yellow Lake), paint the dotted areas, extending the color right to the top or bottom of the flowers, or both, as the case may be. If you look closely at the Color Plate you may be able to see that some of the red parts appear darker than others. These are the parts which will be painted over the transparent yellow. For example, the large red balls along the sides are all painted over the yellow. Wait 24 hours.

4. With a transparent bluish green (Prussian Blue and Indian Yellow), do all the shaded parts. Wait 24 hours.

5. Mix Alizarin Crimson and Indian Yellow with a touch of Burnt Umber, using enough varnish to make a transparent orange red, and go over all the crosshatched parts.

If you should paint this pattern on a box intended as a gift, it would be appropriate to substitute the initials of the recipient.

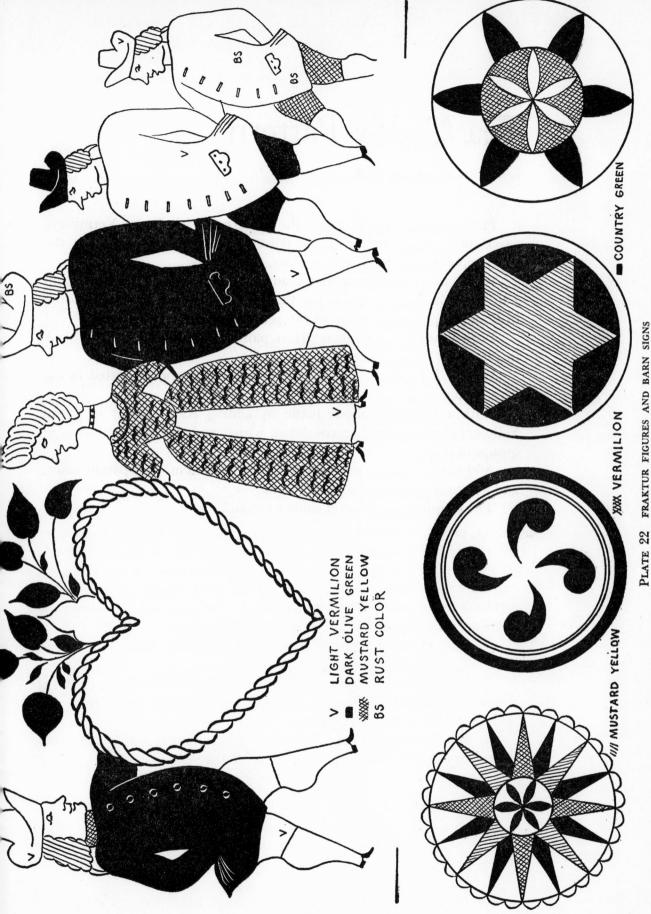

> LIGHT VERMILION
■ DARK OLIVE GREEN
※ MUSTARD YELLOW
BS RUST COLOR

■ COUNTRY GREEN

XXX VERMILION

//// MUSTARD YELLOW

Plate 22 FRAKTUR FIGURES AND BARN SIGNS

Tea Caddy Pattern

Lower half of Line Plate 23

Put a sheet of acetate over the pattern. With Japan Vermilion, paint the over-all shapes of the flowers and fruits, disregarding the superimposed details. Wait 24 hours.

With a dark transparent red, made by mixing Alizarin Crimson and a little Burnt Umber, paint the brush strokes shown by line shading in Plate 23, painting on top of the vermilion.

With a mixture of country green, paint all the parts shown in black in Plate 23. Wait 24 hours.

With a thin off-white, paint the brush strokes shown dotted in the illustration.

With a mustard yellow, made by adding Raw Umber to Japan Yellow, paint the small leaves shown white, and also the large dots in groups of four.

Add varnish to the mustard yellow to get a semi-transparent color, and paint the veins on the green leaves.

The original background color was black.

DARK OLIVE GREEN
MUSTARD YELLOW
V LIGHT VERMILION

V VERMILION
COUNTRY GREEN
DARK TRANSPARENT RED
THIN OFF-WHITE
Y MUSTARD YELLOW

PLATE 23   TWO FRAKTUR FIGURES AND TEA CADDY

[105]

Tower House Pattern

Line Plate 24 — Color Plate X (p. 68)

This pattern was taken from the top of an old Pennsylvania German box owned by the New-York Historical Society. It extended right to the edges. The upper section, with the towered building, was repeated on each of the four sides. The background color is the deep off-white that serves for the sky behind the buildings. To copy the pattern, proceed as follows:

1. Mix some Japan Yellow and Raw Umber to make a mustard yellow. Paint the sections of the buildings which are marked Y in Plate 24; and also the foregrounds, which are the broad bands of yellow extending, in both upper and lower sections, from the buildings down to the dark blue. The green and black in the foregrounds will be painted over the yellow when the latter is dry.

Add a touch of Prussian Blue to the mustard yellow to make a light yellow green, and paint the portions of the buildings marked LG.

With Japan Vermilion paint the roofs and flags, disregarding the heavy black accent lines, which will be put on later. Let the work dry for 24 hours.

2. With a mixture of country green, and disregarding the heavy black parts, paint the tree foliage and the green in the foregrounds. In painting the latter, wipe the brush back and forth on newspaper a few times to get a "dry" brush, one which will achieve the effect shown in the Color Plate X.

Mix some Prussian Blue, Raw Umber, and a touch of White to get dark blue, and paint the blue areas. Again use a "dry" brush to finish off the blue just above the buildings. Wait 24 hours.

3. With transparent Raw Umber, apply the shadows on buildings (shown by the line-shaded areas), doing one at a time, and immediately blending off the left-hand side with a clear varnish brush. Wait 24 hours.

4. With Lamp Black, paint all the heavy black parts.

Mix some Vermilion, Burnt Umber, and White to make a somewhat faded red, and paint the border.

PLATE 24   TOWER HOUSE

Flower Motifs from a
Corner Cupboard

Line Plate 25 — Color Plate XI (p. 68)

These motifs come from an old hand-carved and painted corner cupboard that was made in Switzerland. Used in the Pennsylvania German country, it is a type of early imported art work which inevitably influenced American folk decorators. It is now the property of the New-York Historical Society. The background color for the motifs is a creamy off-white, made by mixing White, Raw Umber, and a little Yellow Ochre.

To make a copy of these patterns on frosted acetate, follow these steps, referring constantly to the Color Plate XI.

Motif A

1. With an off-white mixture, paint the over-all area of the petals, marked W, disregarding the little lines on the petals. With a semi-transparent mustard yellow paint the shaded parts of the larger leaves on the left, immediately blending off the edges with a clear varnish brush. With a thicker mixture of mustard yellow, paint the flower center. Add a little Prussian Blue to the mixture to make a yellow green, and paint the small leaves marked YG. Add more blue to make a regular country green, and paint the crosshatched leaves and stem. Allow 24 hours for drying.

2. With Japan Black, paint all the heavy black accents, veins, and dots. The fine little lines on the petals are in country green.

Motif B

1. Paint the over-all area of the flower in off-white, disregarding all details. With country green, do the crosshatched areas and the tiny stems to the little balls outside the flower. Add some Japan Yellow to this green to make a light yellow green, and paint the large leaf on the right. Wait 24 hours.

[*108*]

W OFF·WHITE
///// MUSTARD YELLOW
▓▓▓ COUNTRY GREEN
YG YELLOW GREEN
P PINK
∴∴ LIGHT BLUE
MB MEDIUM BLUE
■ BLACK

PLATE 25   FLOWER MOTIFS FROM OLD CORNER CUPBOARD

2. With a pale pink, paint the outer edge of the large flower and the little white balls. With a mustard yellow, paint the remaining balls and the center of the flower. Wait 24 hours.

3. With Japan Black, paint the leaf veins and the stamen stems or filaments on the flower. The fine lines on the petals are in a mixture of country green.

Motif C

1. With pale blue, paint the dotted areas. With a mixture of mustard yellow, do the six small shaded brush strokes. Add a little Prussian Blue to make a yellow green, and paint the oval top of the large flower. Add still more blue to make a country green, and paint all the crosshatched leaves and stems. Wait 24 hours.

2. With medium dark blue, paint the area marked MB. With a pale pink mixture, paint the over-all areas marked P, doing first the leaf at the top, and then the lower right-hand flower. Add a little Alizarin Crimson to the mixture to make a darker pink, and *at once* brush in the darker parts on the flower, as shown by the shading lines. Do this immediately before the pale pink has had time to set. Wait 24 hours.

3. With Japan Black, add the black accents and veins.

Motif D

1. With off-white, paint the areas marked W. Add a little Alizarin Crimson and a touch of yellow to this mixture, making a pale pink, and paint the parts marked P. With a mixture of medium blue, paint the flower marked MB. Wait 24 hours.

2. With a mustard yellow mixture, paint the shaded area of the large flower. Add a little blue to make a yellow-green, and paint the leaves marked YG. Add still more blue to make country green, and paint the crosshatched parts. Wait 24 hours.

3. Add the black veins, accents, dots, curlicues, etc.

These motifs were used on the lamp base—fashioned out of a discarded candy tin—which may be seen on p. 88.

Money Box

Line Plate 26 — Sketch Plate A (p. 85)

The original of this box in the museum of the New-York Historical Society has a slot in its lid. It could have been used for coins. The background color is a dark off-white, which is made by mixing White and Raw Umber. The box has a broad stripe of white around the edges of the top and sides. The steps in copying the pattern are:

1. With a mixture of off-white, paint the over-all areas of the birds, the flowers, and the swags of bunting, disregarding all superimposed black and other detail including the shading on the bunting. With dark country green, paint the leaves and stems which are crosshatched in Plate 26. With a mixture of lighter olive green, paint the small leaf strokes shown by fine dots in Plate 26. Let the work dry for 24 hours.

2. With a bright red but thin mixture of Japan Vermilion, paint all the solid black parts on the birds, flowers, and swags, *with the exception of* those flowers marked B. Wait 24 hours.

3. With a slightly transparent dark blue, made by mixing Prussian Blue and Raw Umber, paint the swirls on the flowers marked B. Add the blue brush strokes on the birds, which strokes are indicated by line shading in Plate 26. Also paint the shaded parts of the swags. Now, having wiped the brush back and forth a few times on a piece of newspaper, so as to get rid of most of the paint on it, pick up the merest speck of blue pigment with the flattened brush, and add a few dark accents on the swags to indicate folds.

The birds' eyes also are done in dark blue.

W   OFF-WHITE
XXXX DARK COUNTRY GREEN
LIGHT OLIVE GREEN
VERMILION
B DARK TRANSPARENT BLUE
//// "   "   "

PLATE 26   MONEY BOX

Yellow Candle Box

Line Plates 27, 28, and 29 — Sketch Plate A (p. 85)

This candle box, now in the New York Metropolitan Museum of Art, has a yellow background and a different decoration on each of the five surfaces. Plate 27 gives the strawberry design from the cover, and the designs from the ends of the box. Plates 28 and 29 show the two long side decorations.

The background color is a golden mustard yellow, made by mixing Japan Yellow and some Burnt Sienna. There is no striping on this box.

On all three Plates (27, 28, 29), the areas left white are done in Japan Vermilion. Add a little Burnt Umber to the Vermilion to make it slightly darker. For the line shaded areas in Plates 27 and 29, add a little White to Japan Vermilion to get pink.

The parts shown in black are done in a dark country green. The crosshatched areas are in dark blue. For the dotted areas, indicating large round patches over the vermilion, mix Japan Yellow and Raw Umber to get a mustard yellow which is darker than the background color, and also of a greenish cast in contrast to the background yellow.

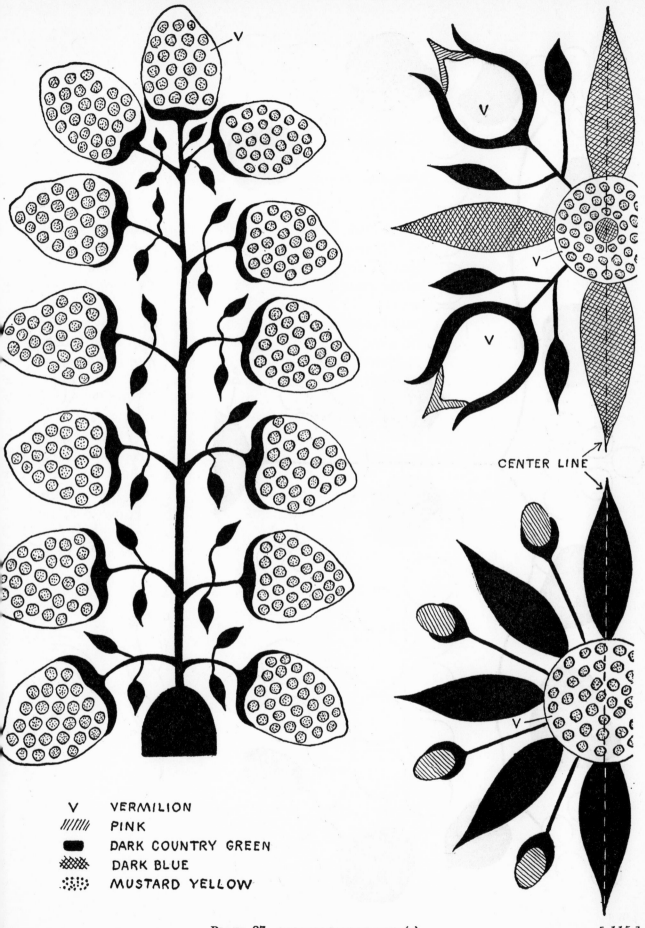

V   VERMILION

//////   PINK

▬   DARK COUNTRY GREEN

▦   DARK BLUE

⁚⁚⁚⁚   MUSTARD YELLOW

CENTER LINE

PLATE 27   YELLOW CANDLE BOX (a)   [115]

PLATE 28 YELLOW CANDLE BOX (b) AND BRUSH—STROKE BORDERS

DARK BLUE

DARK COUNTRY GREEN

PINK

V VERMILION

PLATE 29 YELLOW CANDLE BOX (c) AND BRUSH—STROKE BORDERS

[117]

Decorated Wooden Urn

Line Plate 30 — Color Plate VIII (p. 67)

Although the artist did not sign it, this Pennsylvania German urn, dated 1861, was probably the work of Joseph Lehn, a man who produced many such pieces in the latter half of the 19th century. The other urns shown with this one in the Color Plate VIII are also attributed to Lehn. All are from the collection of Mrs. Huldah Cail Lorimer and are reproduced here by courtesy of the Brooklyn Museum.

Lehn, a retired farmer, began the manufacture and decoration of woodenware as a hobby about 1860. Soon he found that people liked to buy his creations, and for about twenty-five years he turned out many spice chests, egg cups, wooden urns, boxes, tubs, buckets, kegs, and similar things. He is remembered as an outstanding example of the home craftsman and of the folk artist who works in the traditional spirit of his community, producing objects that are both useful and attractive. This champion of folk art against the rising challenge of mass production proved himself a conscientious and capable craftsman. Most of the things he made have withstood the passage of time remarkably well: the colors are still bright, and the finish is more or less intact. Some of Lehn's woodenware, however, was decorated by other artists.

The three motifs lettered A, B, and C in Plate 30 appear in succession around the sides of the urn, and the motif D is one half of the border on the cover. The background color is off-white, now somewhat yellowed with age. To paint the pattern, proceed thus:

1. Mix Japan Vermilion with a little Burnt Umber to make an antique red, and paint the line-shaded areas in motifs B and C. The shading of the strawberries in C is achieved by applying the color to one berry at a time, and then blending off the edge with a varnish brush (see the third paragraph on p. 19), thus leaving a white or unpainted area along one side of each berry, which gives a rounded appearance to the fruit.

With pale pink (obtained by adding White to the above red) paint the narrow band between the edge of the flowers in A and C, and the parallel dotted line. Disregard the dots between these lines.

[*118*]

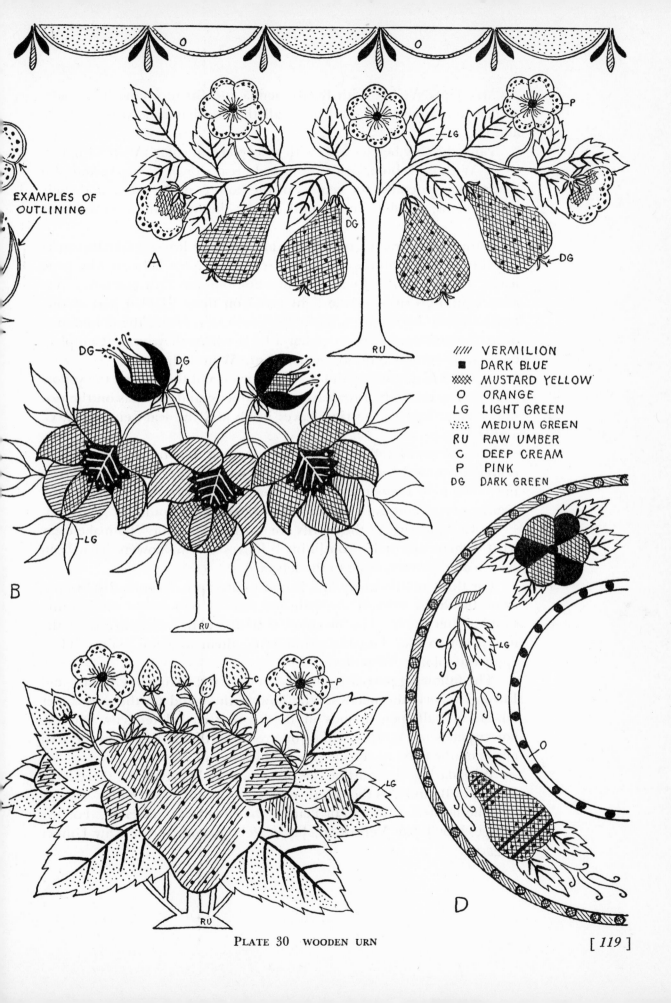

EXAMPLES OF OUTLINING

//// VERMILION
■ DARK BLUE
▨ MUSTARD YELLOW
O ORANGE
LG LIGHT GREEN
∷ MEDIUM GREEN
RU RAW UMBER
C DEEP CREAM
P PINK
DG DARK GREEN

PLATE 30 WOODEN URN

[119]

Mix Japan Yellow with Burnt Sienna and Burnt Umber to make a golden mustard yellow, and paint all the crosshatched parts in A, B, and D.

Paint the tiny berries in C with a deep cream color. Wait 24 hours.

2. With dark blue, paint the broad areas shown in black, and also the following details: the centers of the flowers in A and C, and their tiny stamens; the dots on the pink bands; the heavy lines on the fruit in D.

With light country green, paint all the large leaves in A, B, and D (for the tiny leaves in these and in C, see paragraph 3 below). The large leaves in C are painted with two brushes, one for light green and one for medium green. Use the light green on the unshaded part of one leaf, and then immediately apply the medium green to the dotted area of it; blend the two areas together a little where they meet. Complete one leaf before going on to the next leaf. Wait 24 hours.

3. With dark green, paint the tiny leaves, and the dots on the yellow strawberries in A; the tiny leaves, the stamens, and the dots on the two upper flowers in B; the tiny leaves in C; and the leaf veins in A, C, and D.

With mustard yellow, paint the veins and dots on the blue flower centers in B. With off-white, paint the seed marks on the red berries in C. Mix Raw Umber and White to make a light brown, and paint the stems and tree trunks in A, B, C, and D. Wait 24 hours.

4. Certain parts of the motifs are outlined in color. To make clear what is here meant by "outlining," halves of two flowers have been sketched on a larger scale to the left of A.

For this work you may find it best to use a small pointed #2 water-color brush. The secret in painting with a pointed brush is quite simple: after picking up the color, twirl the hairs of the brush on the newspaper to shape the hairs and bring them to a fine point. Then apply the color to the pattern.

The following parts are outlined in dark red (Alizarin Crimson and Burnt Umber): the petals of the flowers in A and C; the two upper flowers or half-opened buds in B; the tiny curled tendrils, and the flower petals in D. Also, while you are using the dark red, do the seed marks on the five tiny, cream-colored berries in C.

With dark green, outline the yellow and red parts of the three large flowers in B; and also the five tiny, cream-colored berries in C.

The border at the top of Plate 30 has its colors indicated. For the orange, mix Japan Vermilion, Japan Yellow, and a little Raw Umber to make an antique orange. The orange sections are outlined next day with dark green; and the intervening dark green sections are outlined in mustard yellow.

All the motifs in this Plate may be used individually on small boxes, trays, canisters, etc., as well as in combination on bigger pieces.

Oval Trinket Box

Line Plate 31

An oval cedarwood box provides this pattern. The steps in copying are:

1. Mix some Prussian Blue, a little Raw Umber, a touch of White, and a touch of Japan Yellow to make a greenish blue with which you paint all the parts shown in black on Plate 31.

Mix some mustard yellow, adding a touch of White to it, and paint all the shaded areas. Wait 24 hours.

2. With a rather thin mixture of off-white, paint all the strokes shown in white on Plate 31.

There was no striping on this box.

///// MUSTARD YELLOW

■ DARK GREENISH BLUE

'VV OFF-WHITE

PLATE 31 OVAL TRINKET BOX

[123]

Fraktur Birds and a Medallion

Line Plates 32 and 33

The design on Plate 32 is taken from an old Fraktur painting. It is a useful pattern when a vertical motif is needed and is very effectively and easily used for the decorated side of a bread board. Choose a board of very light-colored wood, and proceed as follows:

1. Sandpaper the board and give it a coat of shellac to seal the wood. Allow 24 hours for drying.

2. Sandpaper the surface. Apply a coat of varnish to the side you select for the decoration. Let it dry for 24 hours. The varnish will enable any corrections to be made with Carbona without staining the wood.

3. When varnish is dry, go over it lightly with steel wool, just enough to take off the high gloss. Transfer the design to the board.

Paint the shaded areas, as shown in Plate 32, with a mustard yellow either light enough or dark enough to show easily against the color of the wood, depending on the particular shade of wood your board is made of. Also paint the veins on the center petal of the flower (not those on the side petals). Allow 24 hours for drying.

4. Add a little Burnt Umber to Japan Vermilion, so as to make it slightly darker, and paint all the dotted areas in Plate 32. Also with this color, paint the veins on the two side petals of the flower.

With a very dark country green, paint the crosshatched areas. Dry 24 hours.

5. Using Japan Black, paint the areas shown in black. The birds' eyes are left unpainted.

6. After the usual drying period, finish the decorated surface with one or two coats of varnish.

The designs on Plate 33 of Fraktur birds and a Medallion lend themselves nicely to various objects. Examples are shown on the Sketch C (p. 87)

//////// MUSTARD YELLOW
∷∷∷∷ VERMILION
⨯⨯⨯⨯ DARK GREEN
■ BLACK

PLATE 32   FRAKTUR BIRDS APPLIED TO A BREAD BOARD

A

B

A & B

///// VERMILION
■ DARK GREEN
MUSTARD YELLOW
LEAVES on B · LIGHT GREEN
VEINS on B · BROWN
BS BURNT SIENNA

C & D

W WHITE
///// VERMILION
MUSTARD YELLOW
■ BLACK

C

D

PLATE 33 THREE FRAKTUR BIRDS AND A MEDALLION

[127]

Pennsylvania German Plate

Line Plate 34

The Brooklyn Museum preserves the old plate from which this pattern is taken. The background is a light cream color. The steps in painting the pattern are:

1. Mix a dull olive green, and paint all the crosshatched parts in Plate 34.

Mix some White, Raw Umber, and a little Prussian Blue to make a dull grayish blue, and paint the line shaded areas. Allow 24 hours for drying.

2. Mix some Burnt Sienna with just a touch of White to make it a little more opaque, and paint the parts shown in solid black, the heavy black lines, veins, etc., and also the border. Dry 24 hours.

This pattern is suitable for a round tray or bowl. It should be used only on a light neutral background; for example, on off-white, pale gray, or cream color.

OLIVE GREEN
GRAYISH BLUE
BURNT SIENNA

PLATE 34   PENNSYLVANIA GERMAN PLATE

[129]

Index

The page numbers in italics refer to illustrations.

[*130*]